PUCKS
PABLUM
& PINGOS

PUCKS PABLUM & PINGOS

PUCKS
PABLUM
& PINGOS

MORE FASCINATING FACTS AND QUIRKY QUIZZES FROM CANADA'S TRIVIA GUYS

MARK KEARNEY & RANDY RAY

A HOUNSLOW BOOK
A MEMBER OF THE DUNDURN GROUP
TORONTO

Editorial Director: Anthony Hawke
Copy-Editor: Jennifer Bergeron
Design: Jennifer Scott
Printer: Friesens

National Library of Canada Cataloguing in Publication Data

Kearney, Mark, 1955-
   Pucks, pablum, and pingos : more fascinating facts and quirky quizzes from Canada's trivia guys/
Mark Kearney and Randy Ray.

Includes index.
ISBN 1-55002-500-7

1. Canada — Miscellanea. I. Ray, Randy, 1952- II. Title.

FC61.K445 2004   971'.002   C2004-900457-3

1   2   3   4   5   08   07   06   05   04

Conseil des Arts
du Canada

Canada Council
for the Arts

Canadä

ONTARIO ARTS COUNCIL
CONSEIL DES ARTS DE L'ONTARIO

We acknowledge the support of the **Canada Council for the Arts** and the **Ontario Arts Council** for our publishing program. We also acknowledge the financial support of the **Government of Canada** through the **Book Publishing Industry Development Program** and **The Association for the Export of Canadian Books**, and the **Government of Ontario** through the **Ontario Book Publishers Tax Credit** program, and the **Ontario Media Development Corporation's Ontario Book Initiative.**

Printed and bound in Canada.✪
Printed on recycled paper.
www.dundurn.com

Dundurn Press	Gazelle Book Services Limited	Dundurn Press
8 Market Street	White Cross Mills	2250 Military Road
Suite 200	Hightown, Lancaster, England	Tonawanda NY
Toronto, Ontario, Canada	LA1 4X5	U.S.A. 14150
M5E 1M6		

TABLE OF CONTENTS

INTRODUCTION

So, what the heck is a pingo?

That's just one of the many questions we faced when we started to research this, our seventh book about the quirky side of Canada. And, once we found the answer, we were amazed to discover we weren't the only Canadians who had no clue what a pingo is.

Although we have been researching Canadian trivia for more than a decade, we continue to dig up surprises. Thanks to the success of our previous books, *The Great Canadian Trivia Book* and *The Great Canadian Trivia Book 2*, as well as our other books of Canadiana, we've been inspired to keep on searching far and wide for the weird and wonderful side of this nation.

As you'll discover as you wade through each chapter, we have once again found plenty to write about. If you find this book has something of a random feel to it, you're right. We've grouped many of the items under the chapter headings by common themes, but when there are so many unrelated details, it's almost impossible to find a specific heading for each one. In some cases, we have arranged the items chronologically; in others, we've grouped them in a way that, quite honestly, seemed fun and interesting.

In *Pucks, Pablum & Pingos*, we present trivia in bite-sized chunks so you can flip through at random, discover some amazing oddities, and return later for more. Or, if you'd rather find a comfortable chair and work your way through the entire book in order, that's fine too. We've arranged the book by chapters to make it easy to find the areas that interest you most.

We've also had a ball creating quizzes to test your knowledge of this country, touching on topics we think are dear to the hearts of most Canadians, including the Stanley Cup, literature, beer, the Canadian flag, and automobiles. We think these will be great fun in the car, around the kitchen table, or during idle moments when your mind needs a workout.

Remember, no peeking at the answers until you've made your guess!

In each chapter, we've included sections known as Timelines where, in a sentence or two, we reflect on important events that have taken place in Canada, from goals scored, babies born, and battles won to the opening of buildings, the fall of governments, and the arrival of innovations.

Readers of our previous books have often expressed astonishment at the facts we have unearthed. We're confident that those we present in *Pucks, Pablum & Pingos* will elicit a similar response. And, as always, we hope you'll learn, as we did, how astounding and quirky Canada is, and have fun along the way.

Even better, you'll know what a pingo is.

CHAPTER ONE

HISTORY
HODGEPODGE

BLASTS
FROM
THE
PAST

- The name "Canada" derives from the Huron-Iroquois word "Kanata," which means "village" or "settlement." The term was used to describe Stadacona (the current site of Quebec City) by two Natives who accompanied Jacques Cartier on his 1535 return voyage from France.

- *Where's the beef?* The first crops grown in Canada by non-Natives — cabbages, lettuce, and turnips — were planted by Jacques Cartier circa 1541 in a field in Cap-Rouge, about six kilometres west of Quebec City.

- *Try telling this to snowbirds.* Explorer Samuel de Champlain said of Canada in 1603, "Although Florida may have a more favourable climate than anything I've seen and its soil may be more fruitful, you could hardly hope to find a more beautiful country than Canada."

- The Fortress of Louisbourg, near the eastern tip of Cape Breton Island in Nova Scotia, is the largest historical reconstruction in Canada. The site of Canada's

There's nothing boring about Canadian history.

In fact, there are so many fabulous facts and interesting intricacies from our country's past that it's difficult to decide which ones to include and which ones to leave out.

To tickle your trivia taste buds, we've provided a wide sampling of historical treasures that just might get you to look at Canada from a new perspective.

Courtesy of Nova Scotia Tourism and Culture.

The Fortress of Louisbourg was destroyed in 1760 and later rebuilt.

first lighthouse, the fortress was built in 1713 to protect France's interests in the New World and to serve as the centre of its massive seasonal fishing industry. The American colonies and the British each occupied it for a time before it was blown up in 1760. Reconstruction of approximately one-fifth of the fortress began in 1961 and was completed in 1982.

- Parliament Hill, site of Canada's Parliament Buildings, was purchased after the War of 1812 for just £12. Some years later, the Earl of Dalhousie, then governor of the young British colony that would become Canada, purchased the land for £750. He planned to erect a fort, but a small barracks was all that was built.

Purchased for peanuts: Parliament Hill in Ottawa.

Photo by Andrew Ray.

- *No fiddling around.* Methodists in Upper Canada (now Ontario) once banned the use of violins in playing religious music because of the instrument's association with dancing and merriment. Hey, lighten up!

- Though the British pound was the official currency in Canada from the late eighteenth century until 1858, many different types of currency were used in that period: American dollars, Nova Scotia provincial money, Spanish dollars, and "army bills," which were used by British soldiers in Canada.

- The 202-kilometre Rideau Canal between Ottawa and Kingston was built between 1826 and 1832 to serve as a wartime supply route in case of an invasion by the Americans. But it was never used for its intended purpose and became better known as a route for luxury steamboats. In winter, the City of Ottawa boasts that a 7.8 kilometre section of the canal flowing through the heart of the capital is the world's longest skating rink.

The Rideau Canal is popular with boaters in summer and skaters in winter.

- The Rideau Canal is considered one of the greatest engineering feats of the nineteenth century. Its construction was instigated by the British army under the direction of Col. John By, who wanted to develop an alternative transportation route to the St. Lawrence River, but the job was no easy task; workers fought such killer diseases as malaria and used primitive tools to clear land and do excavating and quarrying.

- "The Maple Leaf Forever," a patriotic song popular among English Canadians in the late nineteenth century and well into the twentieth, was written in 1867 by Alexander Muir as an entry for a poetry contest. It came in second, and Muir later put the poem to music.

- *The battle for ... Kenora?* No shots were fired and no one was killed, but Ontario and Manitoba engaged in a dispute in the late nineteenth century over where the boundaries of each province should be. At

At a dinner meeting in Toronto of the Canadian Manufacturers Association, several speakers advocated the advantages of introducing the metric system to Canada. But this was no recent dinner; it took place in February 1901. The system was not adopted until 1971, and it was not used until April 1975.

one point, in what is now Kenora, Ontario, both Ontario and Manitoba oversaw a municipal government and police force there. Eventually the federal government supported Ontario's land claims.

• The motto "A Mari usque ad Mare" (From Sea to Sea) was first officially used in 1906, when it was engraved on the head of a mace in the Legislative Assembly of Saskatchewan. The phrase was adopted by the federal government in 1921, although another motto, "In memoriam in spem" (In memory, in hope), had also been suggested.

• During the 1920s and '30s as many as fifteen thousand members of the Ku Klux Klan lived in Saskatchewan. The KKK pressured the provincial government to reduce French-language instruction in schools and ban nuns from teaching in the public system.

• Although Americans have been moving to Canada for more than two hundred years, they were not recognized as a distinct ethnic group in the Canadian census until 1991. It's estimated that more than 3 million Americans have immigrated to Canada over the years.

CANADA AT WAR

• *An early separatist movement?* During treaty negotiations between Britain and the United States at the end of the American Revolution, Benjamin Franklin suggested that the British surrender Quebec as a gesture of goodwill. The British refused, but did cede some land south of the Great Lakes.

• Several thousand people living in what is now Canada participated in the U.S. Civil War. The soldiers fought mostly for the North and the cause of opposing slavery, but others fought on the South's side. Some who fought from Canada were former slaves who had escaped into southwestern Ontario.

- During the Civil War, Confederates from the South set up headquarters in Canada. In October 1864, several Confederate soldiers set out from Montreal to raid St. Albans, Vermont, robbed its banks, and returned across the border, where they were free from prosecution. Northern troops threatened to invade Canada in retaliation.

- The Vietnam War was not the first time American soldiers headed north to Canada to escape war duty. Many Americans, labelled "skedaddlers," fled across the border during the U.S. Civil War in the 1860s. So many crossed into an area in New Brunswick that it became known as "Skedaddle Ridge."

- The sinking of the *Lusitania* is associated with Americans and their eventual entry into World War I, but Canadians also suffered losses in the event. When a German submarine near Ireland sank the ship in May 1915, there were 322 Canadians on board. Of them, 175 died, including 82 from Toronto.

- Four of the top ten flying aces in World War I were Canadian: Billy Bishop, Ray Collishaw, Don McLaren, and William Barker.

Oh, by the way, did we tell you the war is over? The Battle of New Orleans, made famous in the 1959 song by American singer Johnny Horton, took place a month after the War of 1812 ended. The British and Americans had signed the Treaty of Ghent, officially ending the war, on December 24, 1814. But it took several weeks for the news to reach military officials, and this final battle took place in January 1815.

Courtesy of the National Archives of Canada, PA-006070.

Canadian air ace William Barker poses with a captured German aircraft in 1919.

During World War I, the Germans and the British referred to Canadian soldiers as "shock troops" after the Canadians proved their worth in a handful of 1917 victories, including those at Vimy Ridge and Passchendale.

- The death of Lt. Alexis Helmer of Ottawa likely inspired John McCrae to write "In Flanders Fields" during World War I. McCrae wrote his famous poem in early May 1915, just hours after his close friend Helmer was killed by a shell on the battle-field at Flanders.

- Canada's legion was born during World War I as the Great War Veterans Association. In 1926 it evolved into the Canadian Legion of the British Empire Services League.

- Lines from John McCrae's famous poem "In Flanders Fields" were used in a series of 1917 advertisements that helped the government's first issue of Victory Loan Bonds raise $400 million for Canada's war effort.

John McCrae and his dog Bonneau.

Courtesy of the National Archives of Canada, C-046284.

- German flyer Manfred von Richthofen, the Red Baron, shot down eighty planes and was considered World War I's greatest ace. Canadian Roy Brown was credited with shooting down the Red Baron in April 1918 in a famous battle in the sky. Recent evidence, however, suggests that anti-air-craft fire from an Australian on the ground killed the Baron.

- Newfoundlander Thomas Ricketts is the youngest soldier to receive the Victoria Cross, the British Empire's highest military honour. Ricketts was seventeen years old on October 14, 1918, when he and his World War I machine-gun crew were pinned down and nearly out of ammunition at Ledeghem, Belgium. A private at the time, he volunteered to run one hundred yards across a fire-swept open field for ammunition and supplies before helping to capture eight guns and eight Germans. For his valour, he was promoted to sergeant and awarded the Victoria Cross by King George V.

Courtesy of the Canadian War Museum.

Thomas Ricketts's medals, prized Victoria Cross at far left.

- When Canada declared war on Japan in World War II, it also ordered the evacuation of all Japanese living within sixty-two kilometres of the British Columbia coast. About twenty-three thousand Japanese were relocated, even though thirteen thousand of them were naturalized Canadian citizens or Canadian born.

- The 1942 shelling of a lighthouse at Estevan Point on Vancouver Island by a Japanese submarine was used as further justification for removing Japanese Canadians from their homes. The Canadian government saw them as a threat to Canadian security during World War II.

- *Women at war.* Approximately fifty thousand Canadian women served their country during

When World War II was declared in 1939, Canada was completely unready, having no tanks, aircraft, or machine guns. While the government placed orders for uniforms and rifles, volunteers trained in their "civvies," sometimes carrying broomsticks.

World War II. Eight-one were killed: six from the Royal Canadian Navy, twenty-five from the army, thirty-two from the Royal Canadian Air Force, ten with nursing services, and eight from the Canadian Merchant Navy.

Postage stamp remembers Canadian women who helped with the war effort.

- Canadian Wally Floody was one of the chief architects of the famous Great Escape of World War II. Floody used his mining expertise from his days in Kirkland Lake, Ontario, to oversee the tunnels being built by prisoners of war at the famous Stalag Luft III camp. Floody didn't get a chance to try out his work because he was moved to another camp before the famous escape took place.

- *Meanwhile, on this side of the ocean …* About thirty thousand German and Italian soldiers were held as prisoners of war in Canada during World War II. One escaped back to Germany to fight again and another got as far as Mexico. A few others got away but never crossed back over the Atlantic Ocean.

- The community of Swastika, Ontario, had no connection to the Nazis, but rather was named for a good luck symbol after gold was found in the area in the early 1900s. Despite efforts by the provincial government during World War II to change the name to Winston, in honour of Winston Churchill, the citizens of Swastika resisted. They argued that the name had been around long before Adolf Hitler appropriated the symbol.

- While Princess Juliana of Holland was taking refuge in Canada during World War II, she gave birth to her third child, Princess Margriet, on January 19, 1943. After the princess's birth, the Dutch flag was flown on the Peace Tower in Ottawa. This was the only time a foreign flag has waved atop Canada's Parliament Buildings.

Just who would have been better at saving Private Ryan, eh? About fifteen thousand Canadians fought alongside American and British soldiers during the D-Day invasion of 1944, and it was the Canadian troops who were the first to reach their planned objective.

- During the Korean War, Canadian soldiers fought in the Battle of Kap'yong in April 1951 and prevented the Chinese from occupying Seoul, Korea. For their efforts, the Canadians received the U.S. Presidential Distinguished Unit Citation for gallantry and heroism.

- The Korean War, which ended in July 1953, claimed 516 Canadian soldiers and left another 1,200 wounded. More than twenty-six thousand Canadians served in Korea.

- In 1960, Queen Elizabeth consented to adding the word "Royal," and the legion became the Royal Canadian Legion, which continues to provide a strong voice for war veterans and advise the government on veterans' issues.

- *And one more thing.* In early 2004, membership in the Royal Canadian Legion was 429,156, including 155 veterans of World War I, 53,591 from World War II, and 3,733 from the Korean War.

QUIZ #1

LEST WE FORGET

The moment of silence that Canadians pause for on the eleventh hour of the eleventh day of the eleventh month is likely the most significant few minutes of time each year in Canada.

Take a few minutes to test your knowledge of Remembrance Day and its significance to Canada and its people.

1. In what year was the first Remembrance Day held throughout the British Commonwealth?

   a) 1918
   b) 1919
   c) 1923
   d) 1931

2. Unscramble the following letters to form the name of the monument that is the site of Remembrance Day ceremonies in many Canadian communities.

   ecntaohp

3. In Canadian poet John McCrae's famous 1915 poem "In Flanders Fields," who or what is Flanders?

   a) Canadian general Charles Flanders, who won a key World War I battle
   b) a Dutch word meaning "farmer"
   c) the Flanders regiment established in Germany in the eighteenth century
   d) a region in Belgium

4. In May 2000, the remains of an unidentified Canadian soldier who died in World War I were returned to Canada and buried in a tomb in front of the National War Memorial in Ottawa. Where were the remains taken from?

   a) France
   b) Belgium
   c) Germany
   d) Great Britain

The tomb of the Unknown Soldier in Ottawa.

5. What happens to the money raised every November during the Royal Canadian Legion's poppy campaign?

    a) It is used to assist veterans and others who took part in wars involving Canadians.
    b) It covers property taxes at legion branches across Canada.
    c) It is donated to the Canadian Armed Forces for equipment.
    d) It is used to maintain cenotaphs in towns and cities across Canada.

Poppies are a familiar sight on jackets and coats around Remembrance Day.

6. Remembrance Day (then called Armistice Day) fell on what holiday throughout the Commonwealth until 1931?

    a) Easter
    b) Thanksgiving
    c) Memorial Day
    d) Labour Day

7. During World War I, what was Private George L. Price's claim to fame?

    a) He was the first Canadian soldier to arrive in France.
    b) He was the last Canadian killed in action before the Armistice took effect at 11:00 a.m. on November 11, 1918.
    c) He was the first Canadian solder to die at Vimy Ridge.
    d) He was the first soldier to wear a poppy on his lapel.

8. What gesture adopted after World War I is still used on Remembrance Day to commemorate those who have given their lives in war?

   a) two minutes of silence
   b) the lowering of flags to half-mast
   c) the closure of outlets that sell alcohol
   d) a conference call between world leaders, including the president of the United States and the prime ministers of Canada and Great Britain

9. In 1931, what did A.W. Neill, an independent MP from British Columbia, contribute to Canada's recognition of its war dead?

   a) He introduced legislation that fixed November 11 as Remembrance Day.
   b) He led a Parliamentary committee that oversaw construction of cenotaphs in many Canadian communities.
   c) He helped initiate the annual sale of poppies in Canada.
   d) He spearheaded a drive to build the Canadian War Museum in Ottawa.

10. The National Silver Cross Mother is chosen annually by the Royal Canadian Legion to take part in Remembrance Day. To do what?

   a) visit war veterans in Canadian hospitals
   b) lay a wreath at the base of the National War Memorial in Ottawa on behalf of all mothers who lost children in the military service of the nation
   c) lobby governments for improved benefits for the children of war veterans
   d) speak with children about the importance of November 11

 Answers found on page 41

MILESTONES

- Henry Hudson was the first European to "discover" James Bay in 1610, but the large body of water in Canada's north didn't get its name until twenty-one years later, when English Captain Thomas James sailed into it and spent a winter there.

- *By the numbers.* Jean Talon, whose title was Intendant of Justice, Police and Finance of New France, conducted the first census in what would eventually become Canada in the winter of 1665–6. He enumerated 3,215 people in the new colony by going door to door and asking questions.

- *We're number two.* Canada was second, after Denmark, to pass legislation against slavery. The law was introduced in 1793, and slavery was fully abolished in 1834.

- The Bank of Montreal, Canada's oldest chartered bank, opened its doors in Montreal in 1817 in a rented building with seven employees and capital amounting to £25,000.

> *En garde.* The first recorded duel in Canadian history took place in Trois-Rivières, Quebec, in 1646 between two French soldiers. They used swords, not pistols, as was the French custom at the time.

- The Yukon Territory was created in June 1898 at the height of the Yukon gold rush in order to assert Canadian sovereignty over the area.

The Bank of Montreal has a strong presence in communities across Canada.

- *A province of firsts.* Nova Scotia can lay claim to a number of firsts in Canada. Sydney Mines was the first town to have dial telephones in 1907, the first powered flight took place at Baddeck in 1909, and Canada's first feature film, *Evangeline*, premiered in Halifax in 1913.

- Though women first got the right to vote in Manitoba in 1916, it took some time for other provinces to follow suit. Women in Newfoundland (not then a province) had to wait until 1925, while their counterparts in Quebec didn't get the right until 1940.

- What do the FLQ and income taxes have in common? Both were affected by the War Measures Act. Although most Canadians identify this legislation with the government's attempts to quell the October Crisis in 1970, the Act, introduced in 1914 by Robert Borden, was used to create income taxes to help raise revenue during World War I. To the disdain of taxpayers from coast to coast, it proved too valuable a cash cow for the government to give up when the war ended a year later.

- The Red Ensign was Canada's recognized flag for many years in the twentieth century, but it was never our country's official banner. The flag was approved for use on government buildings in 1924, and after a lengthy debate the current maple leaf flag replaced it in 1965.

King George V designated the red and white found on Canada's national flag as Canada's official colours in 1921.

The red and white maple leaf flag caused an uproar when it became Canada's official banner in 1965.

- The United Church of Canada was created on June 10, 1925, in Toronto when the Methodist, Presbyterian, and Congregationalist churches of Canada joined forces.

- *Big bang.* On April 5, 1958, the largest non-nuclear peacetime explosion in history took place when Ripple Rock, in Seymour Narrows, Discovery Passage, off the east coast of Vancouver Island, was blown up. Over the years the rock, which lay just beneath the surface of the water, had caused dozens of shipwrecks and taken more than one hundred lives.

- On September 29, 1962, Canada launched the *Alouette I* satellite to study the ionosphere, becoming the third country in space after the Soviet Union and the United States. And when *Apollo 11* touched down on the moon seven years later, it used Canadian-made landing gear.

Canada's first colour television set was set up in an operating theatre at the Royal Victoria Hospital in Montreal on June 21, 1951. It allowed Dr. Gavin Miller to give a running commentary of an abdominal operation.

---

1. True or false? When John Wilkes Booth, the assassin of Abraham Lincoln, was killed during a manhunt, officials found a document from a Canadian bank in Montreal on his body.

2. On which day in 1949 did Newfoundland officially join Canada?

   a) April Fool's Day
   b) Christmas Day
   c) Dominion Day
   d) March 31
   e) May 15

3. Which name was *not* considered for Canada when it officially became a country in 1867?

   a) Cabotia
   b) New Britain
   c) Laurentia

QUIZ #2

TEST YOUR HISTORICAL KNOWLEDGE

Think you know your Canadian history? Try this quiz and see how well you do.

d) Ursalia
e) United States of Canada

4. What West Indian island did some people in Great Britain in the 1760s want to acquire from the French in exchange for Canada?

a) Guadeloupe
b) Haiti
c) Cuba
d) St. Vincent

5. When Louis Riel was executed for staging a rebellion in 1885, what citizenship did he hold?

a) Canadian
b) American
c) British
d) French

6. True or false? There's a bilingual message from former prime minister Pierre Trudeau on the moon that was left by *Apollo* astronauts.

7. Canadian-born Andrew Bonar Law was once prime minister of which country?

a) Canada
b) New Zealand
c) Australia
d) Great Britain
e) South Africa

Answers can be found on page 42

OUR AMERICAN NEIGHBOURS

- The idea of free trade between Canada and the U.S. is nothing new. In 1846, William Hamilton Merritt, a milling and transportation executive, raised the idea of free trade between the U.S. and what would become Canada because he thought companies here would benefit from the larger American market.

- Toronto city council passed a motion in 1865 ordering all Toronto businesses to close for two hours as a way of recognizing the funeral of U.S. President Abraham Lincoln. Council also passed a resolution acknowledging regret for Lincoln's assassination.

> When Canada built its transcontinental railroad in the nineteenth century, the country's population was about 4.5 million. In comparison, the population of the United States when it built its transcontinental railroad was about 37 million.

- William Taft, the twenty-seventh U.S. president, tried to introduce a free trade deal between his country and Canada in the early 1900s, but we turned it down. Taft had another connection to Canada. He had a summer home on what used to be known as Murray Bay, Quebec. Charlie Chaplin also had a home there.

- In 1903, Canada tried to acquire the Alaskan panhandle, which runs along the coast of British Columbia, but an international tribunal of three Americans, two Canadians, and one British representative voted 4 to 2 to award the land to the U.S.

- *Hell no, they didn't go.* Approximately eighty thousand Americans fled to Canada to avoid military service during the Vietnam War. After amnesty was granted, about sixty thousand returned to their homeland.

QUIZ #3

MORE QUIZ-ZICAL QUES-TIONS

A set of trivia teasers to test your Canadian know-how.

1. True or false? In the 1920s, Canada had a plan to invade the United States.

2. In what year did Lester B. Pearson win the Nobel Peace Prize for his work during the Suez Crisis?

   a) 1954
   b) 1956
   c) 1958
   d) 1960

Courtesy of the National Archives of Canada, PA-126393

3. In a national plebiscite in 1898, every province but one favoured intro-ducing prohibition of alcohol to Canada. Which one did not?

   a) Quebec
   b) Ontario
   c) Manitoba
   d) New Brunswick
   e) British Columbia

Lester Pearson won a prize for peace.

4. True or false? Homosexuality was considered a crimi-nal offence in Canada until 1969 and punishable by up to fourteen years in prison.

5. How many times was Sir Isaac Brock, the hero of the War of 1812, buried?

   a) once
   b) twice
   c) three times
   d) four times
   e) Never. He was cremated and the ashes scattered.

6. What early 1990s protest led to the largest mass arrest in Canadian history?

 Answers can be found on page 43

TRAINS AND BOATS AND ... STREETCARS

- Canada's first railway was built in 1836 by brewer John Molson. The Champlain–St. Lawrence Railway linked the Quebec communities of La Prairie and St-Jean.

Beer was not the only claim to fame of John Molson, pictured as a young man at left and a seasoned businessman below.

Courtesy of the National Archives of Canada, C-115899.

© Canada Post Corporation, 1986-87. Reproduced with permission.

- The first steam locomotive manufactured in Canada was built in 1853 by James Good of Toronto. It was named *Toronto* and was part of the great flurry of industrial activity that marked the country's first great railway boom in the 1850s.

- Long before the famed *Bluenose* made its name as the speediest sailing vessel in the world, another Canadian boat, the *Marco Polo*, was capturing the imagination of the seagoing world. Built in New Brunswick in 1851, the *Marco Polo* set the record for fastest trip from Liverpool to Australia and back.

- At the time of Confederation, the Grand Trunk Railway, which ran from Montreal through parts of southern Ontario and included links to the U.S., was the largest railway system in the world.

- When Prince Edward Island joined Canada, the federal government gave it $800,000 to buy back land from absentee landowners, paid off its railway debt, and started a steamer service between the island and the mainland.

- The first electric streetcar system in Canada was installed in Windsor, Ontario, in 1886, whereas Toronto's wasn't in place until 1892. By World War I, forty-eight Canadian cities and towns had streetcar systems.

Streetcars are still a familiar sight in downtown Toronto.

Photo by Mark Kearney.

In 1893, the Canadian Pacific Railroad wanted to build some tracks in Toronto and, in the process, tear down the city's historic Fort York, which had played a prominent role in the War of 1812. The plan was turned down, but in 1916 part of the fort was destroyed for a streetcar line.

- Chinese Canadians, who first came to Canada from San Francisco in search of gold in the 1800s, worked by the thousands on the construction of the western section of the Canadian Pacific Railway. They were often given the most dangerous jobs, such as tunnelling and setting explosives. Historians say three Chinese men died for every kilometre of track that was laid.

- Driver's licences were rare in Canada in 1920. When first-time buyers picked up their vehicles, salesmen often gave them a five-minute lesson on shifting gears and sent them out onto the roads. The first trip home was usually an adventure.

- The *Bluenose*, Canada's most famous ship, was sold in 1942 to a West Indies trading company. Four years later it was wrecked off the coast of Haiti.

Courtesy of the National Archives of Canada, PA-030803.

The *Bluenose* under full sail.

- In 1942, the wooden schooner *St. Roch* became the first ship to sail the Northwest Passage from west to east, taking two years to complete the journey. Two years later, it reversed its trip, sailing east to west. Six years later, it sailed from British Columbia through the Panama Canal to Halifax, thus becoming the first ship to circumnavigate North America.

- When the Canadian Pacific Railway introduced the streamlined, all stainless steel transcontinental train *The Canadian* on April 24, 1955, the rail trip between Montreal and Vancouver was reduced to seventy-one hours and ten minutes. That's sixteen hours less than previous trains took to make the trek.

Courtesy of the National Archives of Canada, PA-175302.

Blowing steam: *The Canadian* sped up cross-Canada rail travel.

QUIZ #4

YOU AUTO KNOW

Test your knowledge of Canada's highways and byways by taking a spin through our auto trivia quiz. Buckle up and keep your hands on the wheel!

1. The McLaughlin Carriage Works in Oshawa, Ontario, founded by the McLaughlin family, evolved into a large Canadian automobile manufacturing company that continues to operate today. Name the company.

2. What do the LeRoy, the Ivanhoe, the Russell, and the Superior have in common?

   a) They're all Canadian-made vehicles.
   b) They were manufactured by Henry Ford in Windsor, Ontario.
   c) They all ran on electric motors.
   d) They're considered the four most valuable cars by collectors today.

3. German automaker Volkswagen ended sales of the Beetle in Canada in 1979. In what year was the Beetle reintroduced in this country?

   a) 1995
   b) 1998
   c) 1994

   The VW Beetle's new look.

4. Name the first two provinces to make wearing seatbelts mandatory.

5. In 1867, Henry Seth Taylor of Stanstead, Quebec, unveiled the first self-propelled, Canadian-built automobile. What was it powered by?

   a) electricity
   b) steam
   c) gasoline
   d) kerosene

Henry Seth Taylor's incredible steam-powered car.

6. The T. Eaton Company raised eyebrows in 1913 by selling one of the following in its popular mail-order catalogue.

    a) tubeless tires
    b) mail-order courses for auto mechanics
    c) automobiles
    d) motor oil in one-quart tins

7. Did Canada's first gasoline filling station open for business in Vancouver or Halifax?

8. Which Canadian province was first to license motor vehicles?

9. The Model T Ford was introduced in 1909. What was the sticker price?

    a) $499
    b) $1,900
    c) $1,150
    d) $475

Model T Ford.

Courtesy of Ford of Canada Archives.

10. What agreement was signed by Canada and the United States in 1965 to create a single North American market for passenger cars, trucks, buses, tires, and automotive parts?

11. I run 820 kilometres from the Quebec border to Windsor, Ontario, and I am spanned by more than five hundred bridges. I am Highway _____.

12. In 1912, a major breakthrough for the gasoline-powered engine was introduced in Canada. What was it?

    a) the electric self-starter
    b) the overhead camshaft
    c) the radiator
    d) a six-cylinder engine block

 Answers can be found on page 44

TRY THESE FACTS ON FOR SIZE

In for a penny, in for a pound. If you think exchange rates for the Canadian dollar are high now, imagine 1858, when the dollar became the official currency of the united Province of Canada. The dollar was defined as 15/73 of the British gold sovereign, which meant the exchange rate to the British pound was $4.86.

Wannabe butter was banned twice.

- Some authorities argue that the Canadian Thanksgiving can be traced to 1578, when explorer Martin Frobisher celebrated surviving a severe storm in the eastern Arctic. But it wasn't until 1957 that the government designated the second Monday in October as the day of the holiday.

- Although cases of malaria are rare in Canada today, the disease was so widespread here in the late eighteenth and early nineteenth centuries that it was considered unusual if a newcomer didn't suffer from it in the first year or two spent in this country.

- Margarine has had a tough time establishing itself in Canada. Lobbying by dairy farmers led to margarine being banned by an Act of Parliament from 1866 to 1917. Butter shortages during World War I led to margarine being legalized, but it was banned again in 1923. Margarine became permanently legal in 1948.

Courtesy of Rodney Boushey, Kilborn Food Market, Ottawa.

- Nova Scotians were so skeptical about joining Canada in 1867 that in the first federal election after Confederation, eighteen of the nineteen MPs elected in that province were separatists. The province asked the British government if it could withdraw from the new country, but the request was turned down.

- As part of the Chinese Immigration Act, 1885, the federal government legislated that every person of Chinese origin who wanted to enter Canada was required to pay $500. This fee was called the "head tax." The tax was so expensive that, in many cases, only one family member could afford the trip to Canada, forcing immigrants to leave wives and children behind. From 1885 to 1923 the government collected an estimated $123 million from this tax, which was abolished in 1923 when the government halted Chinese immigration until 1947.

- Nearly 40 percent of families who settled on the Prairies as farmers in the late 1800s and early 1900s were eventually forced by nature to give up or sell their land. Settlers were discouraged by such challenges as wheat rust, grasshoppers, sawflies, drought, grass fires, hailstorms, and blizzards.

- Though the Klondike gold rush had its roots in the discovery of gold in August 1896, the rest of the world didn't learn about it until almost a year later, when news of the strike reached the west coast via steamship.

> When Canada was being settled in the late 1800s, the Dominion Lands Act promised each new immigrant 160 acres of free land. New arrivals were free to homestead wherever they chose in the west, provided the land was not already taken.

Courtesy of the National Archives of Canada, PA-044919.

Miners digging for Klondike gold.

- In the early 1900s, Chinese newcomers entering Victoria had to wait in a prison called "the Piggery" before being allowed into Canada. The Piggery was torn down in 1978.

- The Ontario government earned $500 million — $5 billion by today's standards — when it took the Dionne quintuplets from their parents and built a special hospital/display centre dubbed "Quintland," where tourists lined up to see the five baby girls born in May 1934 in a farmhouse near North Bay.

The five tiny Dionnes with their mother, Elzire.

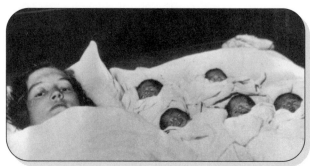

Courtesy of the National Archives of Canada, PA-133260.

- Canadian industrial workers earned twice as much in 1941 as they had just two years earlier in 1939. The need for supplies during World War II greatly reduced the high unemployment that had existed during the Depression.

TIMELINES

January 11	**1909:** The Boundary Waters Treaty signed by Britain and the United States created the International Joint Commission, with U.S. and Canadian members, to settle minor disputes.
January 16	**1906:** Control of the garrison at Halifax was transferred to the Canadian government when the last British soldiers left Canada.
February 1	**1796:** The capital of Upper Canada was transferred from Niagara to York (Toronto).

February 12	**1816:** St. John's, Newfoundland, was almost completely destroyed by a raging fire.
February 18	**1926:** Prohibition officers in New York found 138 cases of champagne under a shipment of potatoes from Prince Edward Island. Canadian potatoes went on the list of suspicious goods being shipped to America.
February 22	**1897:** More than forty Canadians returned to Montreal from Brazil after a failed effort to establish a settlement there. Though promised riches, the Canadians suffered from tropical diseases and found Brazil natives to be inhospitable.
March 7	**1908:** The University of British Columbia was founded as a branch of McGill University. UBC became an independent university in 1915.
March 18	**1918:** Daylight Savings Time was first used.
March 27	**1834:** William Lyon Mackenzie was elected the first mayor of Toronto. Three years later he would lead a failed rebellion against the government of Upper Canada.
April 1	**1975:** The first use of the metric system in everyday Canadian life began with temperature announcements in Celsius. The national process of converting from imperial to metric measures was completed by 1983.
April 9	**1917:** Canadian soldiers began attacking the German stronghold at Vimy Ridge. Six days later the Canadians won the battle, the most significant military victory in Canada's history.

Courtesy of the National
Archives of Canada, PA-1187.

**Victory at Vimy
Ridge brought fame
to Canada's troops.**

April 29

1903: At 4:10 a.m. between 70 and 90 million tons of limestone from Turtle Mountain crashed onto the town of Frank, Alberta, and a nearby valley, killing at least seventy people. It was Canada's most destructive landslide.

May 19

1904: A fire that began on Wellington Street swept through Toronto's downtown, destroying one hundred buildings and causing more than $10 million in damage. No one was killed, and the city rebuilt its core in the years leading up to World War I.

May 24

1881: The steamer *Victoria* sank in the Thames River in London, Ontario, with 181 lives lost. The overloaded boat was bringing Victoria Day celebrants home from festivities in a city park.

May 29

1914: The Canadian Pacific steamer *Empress of Ireland* collided with the Norwegian ship *Storstad* in the Gulf of St. Lawrence and sank. It was the worst marine disaster in Canadian history, claiming 1,012 lives.

June 13

1898: The Yukon was created as a territory. The gold rush that had begun two years earlier brought prospectors from around the world and made Dawson at the time the largest city west of Winnipeg and north of San Francisco.

June 17

1919: Eight of the Winnipeg General Strike leaders were arrested. The most famous general strike in Canada's history shut down the city for six weeks.

Courtesy of the National Archives of Canada, PA-163001.

Strikers made history when they swarmed Winnipeg's streets in 1919.

June 12	**1849:** Twelve people were killed in a riot between Orangemen and Catholics in Saint John, New Brunswick.
June 18	**1812:** American President James Madison declared war on Great Britain and thus launched the War of 1812. The conflict lasted more than two years and became a key development in Canada's history.
July 24	**1534:** Explorer Jacques Cartier erected a cross on the Gaspé Peninsula and claimed Canada for France.
August 1	**1834:** Close to one million slaves were freed in the British Empire as slavery was abolished. There were few slaves in British North America, as the practice had been slowly dying out.
August 3	**1876:** The first telephone call from one building to another took place between Alexander Graham Bell at Mount Pleasant, Ontario, and his uncle David Bell at nearby Brantford.
August 13	**1906:** Norwegian explorer Roald Amundsen reached Nome, Alaska, in the Goa after the first east-to-west navigation of the Northwest Passage. Amundsen began his voyage on June 17, 1903.
August 23	**1797:** The last slave transaction in Canada was made at Montreal, where Emanuel Allen was sold at public auction.
September 7	**1969:** The Official Languages Act, which mandated that a variety of government notices, orders, and services be provided in both English and French, came into effect.
September 17	**1974:** The first female RCMP recruits began training at Regina.
October 5	**1813:** The great chief Tecumseh died at the Battle of Moraviantown in southwestern Ontario. Tecumseh had scored several victories over the Americans up to that point, and many considered his loss a low point in the War of 1812.

October 14   **1968:** Led by René Lévesque, the Parti Québécois was formed, its purpose to bring about the separation of Quebec from Canada.

Courtesy of the National Archives of Canada, PA-115039.

Canada's separatist premier.

November 7   **1885:** Lord Strathcona drove the last spike in a ceremony at Craigellachie, British Columbia, thus completing the Canadian Pacific Railway. The spike was made of iron, not silver or gold as some have thought.

Courtesy of the National Archives of Canada, PA-115039.

The Last Spike.

November 9   **1965:** Thirty million people in the northeastern region of Canada and the United States were plunged into blackness by a power outage known as the Great Northeast Blackout. The official investigation blamed the malfunction of equipment near Niagara Falls, Ontario, for causing a sudden power surge.

November 23   **1815:** The first streetlamps in Canada were installed in Montreal, fuelled by whale oil.

December 17   **1864:** For the first time, passports were required to enter the U.S. from British North America.

QUIZ #1: LEST WE FORGET

1. b) 1919. Originally called Armistice Day, it commemorated the end of World War I on Monday, November 11, 1918, at 11:00 a.m.

2. Cenotaph.

   The cenotaph is the monument Canadians gather around to remember those who fought in past wars.

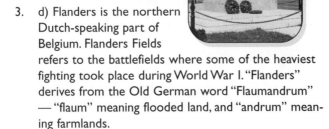

3. d) Flanders is the northern Dutch-speaking part of Belgium. Flanders Fields refers to the battlefields where some of the heaviest fighting took place during World War I. "Flanders" derives from the Old German word "Flaumandrum" — "flaum" meaning flooded land, and "andrum" meaning farmlands.

4. a) France, in the vicinity of Vimy Ridge. The Tomb of the Unknown Soldier honours more than 116,000 Canadians who sacrificed their lives in the cause of peace and freedom.

5. a) It is a major source of funds to assist veterans, ex-service people, their dependents, and veterans' charities with medical assistance and equipment, meals, transportation, shelter, clothing, and disaster relief.

6. Thanksgiving. Both were held on the Monday of the week in which November 11 fell. In 1931, following a decade of lobbying by veterans' organizations, the government changed the name from Armistice Day to Remembrance Day and placed it on November 11, the anniversary of the day World War I ended.

7. b) Price was the last Canadian killed in action, shot by a German sniper only minutes before the Armistice took effect, ending World War I.

8. a) The ritual two minutes of silence was adopted in Canada and other countries in 1919 when King George issued a proclamation.

9. a) Neill introduced the Armistice Day Amendment Act, which fixed November 11 as Armistice Day. Before the Act passed, another MP from B.C., Conservative C.H. Dickie, introduced an amendment that renamed the day Remembrance Day.

10. b) She lays a wreath at the base of the National War Memorial on behalf of all mothers who have lost children in wars.

QUIZ #2: TEST YOUR HISTORICAL KNOWLEDGE

1. True. Booth had spent time in Montreal a few months earlier plotting with Confederate soldiers and had opened a bank account there.

2. d) March 31. Newfoundland was originally set to enter Confederation on April 1, 1949, but Premier Joey Smallwood got the date pushed back a day to avoid any possible jokes about joining on April Fool's Day.

Courtesy of the National Archives of Canada, PA-113253.

Joey Smallwood was no April Fool.

3 e) United States of Canada. All the others and more were considered.

4. a) Guadeloupe. Though few took them seriously, they argued that the island's coffee and sugar crops would be better for Britain economically than Canada's fur trade.

5. b) American. That's why some people felt he shouldn't have been found guilty of treason toward Canada.

6. True. The English part of the message reads, "Man reached out and touched the tranquil moon," while the translation of the French portion is "May that high accomplishment allow man to rediscover the earth and there find peace."

7. b) Great Britain. In 1922, former cabinet minister Law served 209 days as prime minister before resigning because of ill health.

QUIZ #3: MORE QUIZZICAL QUESTIONS

1. True. The plan was devised by a secretary of defence but few took him seriously.

2. b) 1956. Pearson, who was then secretary of state for External Affairs, proposed to the United Nations that an international peacekeeping force be employed to monitor a cease-fire in the area.

3. a) Quebec. The Liberal government under Wilfrid Laurier refused to introduce the legislation for fear of damaging French-Canadian political support.

4. True. The law was amended that year to allow homosexual acts between two consenting adults aged twenty-one and older. The age of consent for oral sex was later lowered to fourteen.

5. d) Four times. Brock was first buried in a fort, then in the old Brock monument, then in a temporary grave after that monument was damaged in an explosion, and he was finally laid to rest under the current Brock monument.

6. It was the anti-logging protests at Clayoquot Sound, B.C. More than 900 protestors were arrested and 857 charged with contempt of court.

QUIZ #4: YOU AUTO KNOW

1. General Motors of Canada.

2. a) They were all Canadian-made vehicles.

3. b) 1998.

4. Ontario and Quebec both made wearing seatbelts mandatory in 1976.

5. b) Steam.

6. c) Automobiles.

7. Vancouver.

8. Ontario began to license automobiles in 1903.

9. c) $1,150.

10. It was the Canada–U.S. Automotive Products Agreement, or the Autopact, for short.

11. 401.

12. a) The electric self-starter.

CHAPTER TWO

FLICKS FACTS

- Twenty Canadian-born actors and actresses have been nominated for Academy Awards during the more than seventy-year history of the Oscars. And the winners were … Mary Pickford, Norma Shearer, Marie Dressler, Deanna Durbin (special award), Walter Huston, Harold Russell, and Anna Paquin.

Mary Pickford, a Toronto native known as America's sweetheart.

Courtesy of the National Archives of Canada, C-16958.

- The first movie star was Canadian. Actors weren't given onscreen credit in movies' early days until Florence Lawrence of Hamilton, Ontario, came along. In 1910, thanks to a publicity stunt, the actress became known as the "Biograph Girl," thus introducing the star system in movies.

- Toronto-born actress Beatrice Lillie was often billed as "the funniest woman in the world." In addition to starring in several stage plays by Noel Coward, the comedienne appeared in several films from the silent era up until her last film in 1967, *Thoroughly Modern Millie*.

- Canada's National Film Board won its first Academy Award in 1941 for the documentary *Churchill's Island*. The NFB has received many nominations and wins over the years, including a special award to commemorate its fiftieth anniversary.

Don't touch that dial or turn that page. When it comes to entertainment, Canadians don't take a back seat to anyone.

Throughout the decades, they've made their marks in front of and behind the camera, at the microphone and the producer's console, in books and comics, in galleries, on stage, and in the wings.

We hope you'll find the following as entertaining as the people we're writing about.

- Toronto and Vancouver each lay claim to the title "Hollywood North" because of the number of films shot in those places, but the small town of Trenton, in eastern Ontario, can boast that it earned the title first. Studios built in 1916 attracted many renowned filmmakers, and several silent movies were shot in the community until the early 1920s. The Ontario government later purchased the studios and made films there until 1934.

- Although moviegoers are familiar with the subtitles that run on foreign films, the idea goes back to silent film days and a system created by Canadian-born director Al Christie. Usually action would take place, followed by a screen of captions. Christie's idea was to print dialogue along the bottom of the film that coincided with the action on the screen.

The site of Canadian Al Christie's studio in Hollywood is now occupied by the CBS network.

- Denys Arcand, the Quebec director best known for his films the *Decline of the American Empire* and *Jesus of Montreal*, started in the business with the National Film Board. In 1970, he made a documentary on the textile industry, *On est au coton*, that was so controversial that it was suppressed for six years.

- Canada's first drive-in movie theatre is believed to have opened in Stoney Creek, Ontario, on July 10, 1946. It was called The Skyway, and its first featured movie was *Casanova Brown*.

YOURS FOR A SONG

- The oldest Gilbert & Sullivan society in Canada is the West Montreal Operatic Society. Formed in 1939, the society gave its first Gilbert & Sullivan performance in 1940 and has done an annual production of operettas ever since.

- The first Canadian singer to have a number one hit on Toronto's famous CHUM Chart was Paul Anka, of Ottawa, Ontario. "Diana" hit number one in August 1957 and was also number one on the U.S. Billboard charts. The next Canadian to top the chart was Jack Scott of Windsor, Ontario, with his song "My True Love" in 1958.

Organ music was first heard in Canada in a Quebec church in the early 1660s, about sixty years before a similar event took place in the U.S. Most organs were imported from Europe, but the first Canadian-built instrument was completed in 1723.

Toronto's famous CHUM Charts were the bible of the Canadian record industry in the fifties and sixties.

- Before his first smash hit "Diana" was released in 1957, Paul Anka recorded a song called "I Confess" in California that flopped. He told *Maclean's* magazine that the record company failed to promote the song and that the record made him a measly $1.82.

Anka's "Diana" was no flop.

• Sandy Gardiner, a former Ottawa journalist now living in Florida, is credited with coining the word "Beatlemania" to describe the frenzy created by the 1960s British rock group. He came up with the term while covering the Beatles during a trip to Liverpool in the Fab Four's early days.

Sandy Gardiner is Canada's connection to the term "Beatlemania."

Courtesy of Sandy Gardiner.

• The authorship of the famous World War I song "Mademoiselle From Armetières" is often disputed, but one of its co-writers was possibly Gitz Ingraham Rice of New Glasgow, Nova Scotia.

• Guy Lombardo, famous Canadian bandleader from the 1920s to the '70s, performed mostly with a baton in his hand. But he started out as a violin player and often used his bow to lead the band.

The "sweetest music this side of heaven" can still be heard at the Guy Lombardo Museum in London, Ontario.

• Canadian singer-songwriter Bryan Adams was born in Kingston, Ontario, but before moving to Vancouver as a fifteen-year-old, he also lived in England, Israel, Portugal, and Austria. He has sold more than 60 million records worldwide.

- Musician Bobby Gimby earned the nickname "the Pied Piper of Canada" for his Centennial song, "Ca-na-da," which featured the voices of young Canadians, but it wasn't his only nationalistic song. Gimby was commissioned in the 1960s to write a song commemorating the founding of Malaysia, and the result was "Malaysia Forever."

Photo courtesy of the late Bobby Gimby.

Bobby Gimby was an all-around musical talent best known for the song "Ca-na-da."

- Buffalo Springfield, a U.S.-based 1960s rock band featuring Canada's Neil Young, took its moniker from the company name printed on the side of a steamroller the band spotted at the side of the road. "Wouldn't it be groovy if we ever got as big as that steamroller?" a member of the band joked at the time.

- Dewey Martin, one of the few Canadians in the Rock and Roll Hall of Fame, earned that distinction as Buffalo Springfield's drummer. But long before he joined that band, Martin had earned a reputation as a top session drummer in Nashville, playing with such country stars as Patsy Cline, Carl Perkins, and Faron Young.

Photo by Catherine Blake.

Several Canadian musicians have been inducted into the Rock and Roll Hall of Fame in Cleveland.

"Born to be Wild," the 1960s rock hit by Canadian group Steppenwolf, was written by band member Dennis Edmonton (a.k.a. Mars Bonfire) after he drove a motor-cycle through San Francisco one night. According to one band member, that was the first time Bonfire had ever driven a motorcycle.

- Singer Anne Murray of "Snowbird" and "Can I Have This Dance?" fame has won twenty-five Juno Awards in her long career. Add in Grammy Awards and countless other prizes she's won, and that's plenty of musical hardware.

- Gene Cornish of Ottawa was the lead guitarist of the successful 1960s band the Rascals. Known for such hits as "Groovin'," "A Beautiful Morning," and "People Got to Be Free," the New York-based group, including Cornish, was inducted into the Rock and Roll Hall of Fame in 1997.

- Though many have panned the song, Dan Hill's "Sometimes When We Touch" was not only a number one hit in Canada, it also topped the charts in eleven other countries. It reached number three on the U.S. Billboard chart in late 1977.

- *A great track record.* During his career, record producer Jack Richardson of Toronto, who has been named a member of the Order of Canada for his work with the Guess Who, Alice Cooper, Bob Seger, and others, produced twenty-seven Billboard charted singles, more than twenty charted albums, and received thirty-eight gold and platinum awards.

When the Guess Who recorded "These Eyes," they had to be convinced to release it as a single. Guitarist Randy Bachman remembers, "We didn't want to be a ballad band. We wanted to take prairie rock to the world." Fortunately, the band agreed, the song hit the top ten, and it has since become one of the most played Canadian songs on the airwaves ever.

- Songwriter Pierre Senecal says it took him only fifteen minutes to write the 1970 hit song "As Years Go By" for his Montreal-based band Mashmakhan. The tune reached number one in Canada and the top forty in the U.S., and was one of the biggest selling singles ever in Japan.

- When Scarborough, Ontario-based Ocean recorded the song "Put Your Hand in the Hand," band members were hoping it would lead to better-paying gigs on the high school circuit. In fact, it did a lot more, as the song rocketed to number two on the Billboard charts in 1971.

- So how did Bachman become so proficient on the guitar? He used to play guitar in the dark without looking at his frets. When he was a youngster his dad would holler "lights out" at night, and Bachman would keep on practising.

- One of Canadian rocker Neil Young's first jobs in the music industry was as a deejay at the Earl Grey Community Club in Winnipeg. His first band played at the same club.

- Songwriter Terry Jacks offered his tune "Seasons in the Sun" to Toronto band Edward Bear, which turned it down. In return, the band offered "Last Song" to Jacks but he declined. Both recorded their own songs and enjoyed number one hits with them.

> Randy Bachman, lead guitarist with Canadian bands Bachman-Turner Overdrive and the Guess Who, in 2004 owned a collection of about 380 Gretsch guitars valued at more than $2 million. Bachman, who plays a Gretsch himself, is known in music circles as the "Gretsch Guy."

Larry Evoy's success in music allowed him to enjoy this rural retreat near Toronto.

Photo by Mark Kearney.

- Susan Jacks, singer in the 1960s group the Poppy Family, debuted professionally at age fourteen at a dance in Haney, British Columbia, where she was paid one dollar. She later had a string of hits, including "Which Way You Goin' Billy?" and "That's Where I Went Wrong."

- Folksinger David Bradstreet, who once won a Juno Award for Most Promising Male Vocalist, tried to sell the statue years later at a garage sale. Of

David Bradstreet, with guitar in hand and tongue in cheek, once attempted to sell his Juno.

course, his tongue-in-cheek price tag of fifteen thousand dollars didn't attract any buyers.

• In March 1965, "Shakin' All Over," by Winnipeg's the Guess Who, roared up the Canadian music charts to displace the Beatles' "Eight Days a Week" at number one. It was among the first songs by Canadian performers to break out of the regional music scene and become a number one record across the country.

• St. Michael's Choir in Toronto was the birthplace of many successful pop musicians. The Crew-Cuts, the Four Lads, and the Diamonds, three singing groups who had smash international hits in the 1950s, all got their start there.

Courtesy of the Crew-Cuts.

The Crew-Cuts were just one of the groups that made it big after singing in St. Michael's choir.

When Canadian singer Alanis Morissette was three years old, she memorized songs from the movie *Grease* and, using a nail polish bottle for a microphone, belted out those songs and others for anyone willing to listen.

• Country singer Wilf Carter, who hailed from Nova Scotia, enjoyed popularity in the U.S. beginning in the 1930s. Despite his Canadian origins, his stage name south of the border was "Montana Slim."

• Canadian Frank Mills's piano tune "Music Box Dancer" was not only a huge hit for the composer, it also sold more than 2 million copies of sheet music worldwide. That made it the biggest selling song sheet for many years.

DID YOU KNOW. . .

- "O Canada" was first performed on June 24, 1880, in Quebec City with French lyrics. Various English lyrics were written before the ones Canadians are familiar with caught on in 1908.

- Although Superman was depicted as fighting for truth, justice, and the American way, he was co-created by a Canadian. Toronto-born Joe Shuster created the Man of Steel in the 1930s with his American friend Jerry Siegal.

The Man of Steel fought for the American Way, but he had Canadian roots.

Canadian Thomas (Doc) Kelley may have invented the pie in the face gag. In 1889, he and others laughed when a stable boy in Newfoundland got hit on the shirt with a pie. Kelley concluded that a pie in the face would be even funnier, and the gag became an entertainment staple for decades.

- Hal Foster of Halifax, Nova Scotia, was a catalogue illustrator for Eaton's and the Hudson's Bay Company early in his career. He gained worldwide fame in 1937 when he created the Prince Valiant comic strip, still read by millions today.

- *Punch in Canada*, which was named after the famous humour magazine in Britain, was the first publication in Canada to regularly feature cartoons. Launched in 1841 by John H. Walker, the publication folded about ten years later when he tried to publish it weekly.

Hollywood continues to be the centre of the movie world long after Canadian director Al Christie directed the first film there.

Photo by Mark Kearney.

- About 4.6 million Canadians aged fifteen or older read at least one book a week, but another nine hundred thousand read only one book a year, according to Statistics Canada.

- London, Ontario's Al Christie is credited with making the first film ever in Hollywood, *The Law of the Range,* in 1911. Another account, however, says the first Hollywood film was Christie's *The Best Man Wins.* Regardless, it was the start of a long career as a director/producer. By 1916, he had his own film studio, the Christie Film Company, which he ran with his brother Charles.

- Toronto's Factory Theatre, founded in 1970, was the first English-language theatre in Canada to devote itself exclusively to Canadian scripts. Plays in its first season included *Creeps,* by David Freeman, and *Esker Mike and His Wife, Agiluk,* by Herschel Hardin.

- The Edmonton Fringe Festival is the largest alternative theatre event in North America. The ten-day summer festival attracts almost half a million theatregoers each year.

Edmonton has more professional theatre companies per capita than any other major city in Canada. Its nineteen theatre companies represent a rate of 2.2 companies per 100,000 people. In comparison, Toronto's rate is 1.43 per 100,000.

1. The first book to win the Governor General's Award for Non-Fiction was a collection of columns by T.B. Robertson. Which newspaper did he write for?

   a) *Toronto Telegram*
   b) *Ottawa Citizen*
   c) *Winnipeg Free Press*
   d) *Halifax Daily News*

2. The only Canadian movie to win Genie Awards for Best Actor, Best Actress, Best Supporting Actor, and Best Supporting Actress was:

   a) *Long Day's Journey into Night*
   b) *Mon Oncle Antoine*
   c) *Goin' Down the Road*
   d) *Jesus of Montreal*

3. Paul McCartney of the Beatles wore the badge of this Canadian police force in a photo on the *Sgt. Pepper* album. Which one was it?

   a) the RCMP
   b) the Ontario Provincial Police
   c) Metro Toronto Police
   d) Montreal Police Force

4. True or false? Louis B. Mayer, the film producer who grew up in New Brunswick, was responsible for creating the Academy Awards.

5. The first photographs ever taken in Canada were believed to be shots of what famous Canadian site?

   a) the Parliament Buildings
   b) Halifax Harbour
   c) the Chateau Frontenac
   d) Lake Louise
   e) Niagara Falls

6. What Toronto rock band from the 1970s was thought to be the Beatles reunited?

   a) Liverpool

QUIZ #5

AN ENTER-TAINING QUIZ

Culture vultures will find a taste of all sorts of entertainment in this eight-question quiz.

b) The Four Lads
c) Klaatu
d) Fludd

7. Before he joined the Guess Who, Burton Cummings was lead singer of which Winnipeg band?

    a) The Deverons
    b) The Expressions
    c) The Squires
    d) The Staccatos

8. Douglas Shearer of Montreal and Richard Day of Vancouver hold the honour of being the Canadians who have won the most Academy Awards. How many did each win during their long Hollywood careers behind the cameras?

    a) four
    b) seven
    c) nine
    d) twelve

Answers can be found on page 68

TALES FROM THE TUBE

*   The comedy team Wayne and Shuster, who were legends in the history of Canadian entertainment, appeared a record sixty-seven times on the *Ed Sullivan Show*, which was broadcast on Sunday nights on CBS television from 1948 to 1971.

Johnny Wayne and Frank Shuster were stalwarts on the *Ed Sullivan Show*.

Courtesy of the National Archives of Canada, PA-152117.

56

- *Reach for the Top*, a Canadian high school TV quiz program, started in Vancouver in 1961. It spread to Edmonton the next year and eventually was broadcast across the country. When CBC threatened to dump the program in 1983, protests reached all the way to the House of Commons. The show finally ended its run in 1985.

- Long before he gained renown as Pa Cartwright on the TV series *Bonanza*, Canadian-born actor Lorne Greene made a name for himself as a radio broadcaster. During World War II he was known to CBC listeners as the "Voice of Doom."

> Game show host Alex Trebek may be Canada's most famous quizmaster today, but another Canadian, Roy Ward Dickson, gets credit for inventing the genre. His radio program *Professor Dick and his Question Box* debuted in Toronto on May 15, 1935.

Courtesy of the National Archives of Canada, PA-116178.

Lorne Greene: from Voice of Doom to cowboy.

- The Viewer Chip, or V-Chip, used by parents to block violent or offensive television shows from coming into their homes, was invented by Tim Collins, a professor at the Technical University of British Columbia in Surrey, British Columbia.

- Joan Miller of Nelson, British Columbia, made history in November 1936 when she appeared on a British Broadcasting Corporation program. As the "Picture Page Girl," Miller was paid £12.10 per

> The Canadian TV show *Hammy Hamster*, which debuted in 1959, is still seen in more than twenty countries around the world.

week, making her television's first professional performer. She later made a name for herself as one of Britain's greatest stage actresses.

Actor Matthew Perry, one of the stars of the *Friends* TV sitcom, first performed before an audience while studying at Ashbury College in Ottawa, where he played the fastest gun in the West in a play called *The Life and Death of Sneaky Fitch*. He lived in Ottawa until he was fifteen; his mother, Suzanne Perry, was former prime minister Pierre Trudeau's press secretary.

In the 1950s, CBC ran a Canadian version of the popular American show *Howdy Doody*. Instead of using American host Buffalo Bob, the CBC came up with Timber Tom, a forest ranger, who was played in a few episodes by future *Star Trek* star William Shatner. Interestingly, the role of Timber Tom had been first offered to James Doohan, who would later play Scotty on *Star Trek*.

- Before he made it really big in stand-up, comedian Steve Martin spent a year as a regular on the Canadian-made program *Half the George Kirby Comedy Hour*, which was produced at CTV in Toronto in 1972–73.

BOOK BITS AND BITES

- Irving Layton is considered one of Canada's greatest poets, but based on what he studied at university you wouldn't think rhyming couplets would have been his career. He earned a bachelor of science in agriculture and did graduate work in political science.

- Saul Bellow won the Nobel Prize for literature in 1976. Though born in Lachine, Quebec, in 1915, he had lived in the United States since he was nine and was an American citizen when he won the award.

- Leslie McFarlane of Haileybury, Ontario, wrote the first twenty books in the famous Hardy Boys series under the pen name Franklin W. Dixon. They were among the best-selling boys' books of their time, but McFarlane received no royalties.

Photo by Catherine Blake.

The Hardy Boys were popular with many young Canadian readers.

• *Anne of Green Gables*, the story of the little red-haired orphan from Prince Edward Island, written by Lucy Maud Montgomery, was first published in 1908 and is considered the best-selling Canadian book of all time.

Though Lucy Maud Montgomery is best known for her *Anne of Green Gables* books, the prolific author also published some 450 poems and 500 short stories during her illustrious career.

• Before he found success with his novel *Who Has Seen the Wind*, W.O. Mitchell made a living as a labourer, door-to-door salesman, and part-time teacher. The 1947 novel was so successful that Mitchell made his living exclusively as a writer from then on.

• Coles Notes, the helpful guides to literature, were first introduced in 1948. The first booklet was for a French novella called *Colomba*, while *The Merchant of Venice* was the first Shakespearean play to get the Coles treatment.

More than a few Canadian students were able to pass their English literature exams thanks to Coles Notes.

Photo by Catherine Blake.

• The celebrated book *Uncle Tom's Cabin* is loosely based on the experiences of Reverend Josiah Henson. The former Maryland slave escaped to Upper Canada via the Underground Railroad and set up a farming community in 1841 near what is now Dresden, Ontario.

The real Uncle Tom's Cabin, the home of former slave Josiah Henson near Dresden, Ontario.

- Arthur Hailey, one of the world's best-selling authors, got the idea for his popular novel *Airport* while being shown around a new section of Toronto International Airport (now Lester B. Pearson International Airport) by its designer, John Parkin.

The Governor General's and Juno awards have both been won by novelist/poet/songwriter Leonard Cohen. He has three Junos and won the Governor General's Award in 1968 for his novel *Beautiful Losers*.

QUIZ #6

LITERARY QUIZ

This shouldn't be the only book you ever crack open. If you're a fan of Canada's rich literary tradition, wrap your brain around some of these publishing ponderables.

1. This famous poet once appeared in a film with John Wayne and Marlene Dietrich. Who was it?

   a) Irving Layton
   b) Raymond Souster
   c) Robert W. Service
   d) Earle Birney

2. The first Governor General's Award for Fiction went to which author?

   a) Gabrielle Roy
   b) Morley Callaghan
   c) Sinclair Ross
   d) Bertram Brooker

3. Robertson Davies' Deptford trilogy is made up of *Fifth Business*, *World of Wonders*, and what other book?

   a) *Leaven of Malice*
   b) *The Manticore*
   c) *The Rebel Angels*
   d) *Tempest-Tost*

4. Which Timothy Findley novel tells the story of the momentous battle between Jung, self-professed mystical scientist of the mind, and his suicidal patient?

5. *This Side Jordan,* published in 1960 and set in Ghana, was which Canadian author's first novel?

6. What is the name of the town that is the setting of several Margaret Laurence novels, including *The Stone Angel* and *A Jest of God?*

   a) Maniwaki
   b) Manawaka
   c) Minaki
   d) Moonstone

7. Poet and children's author Dennis Lee once co-wrote songs for which TV program?

   a) *Sesame Street*
   b) *Fraggle Rock*
   c) *Mr. Roger's Neighborhood*
   d) *Mr. Dressup*

8. Margaret Atwood and George Bowering are among the three Canadian English writers who have won the Governor General's Award in both the fiction and poetry categories. Name the third.

9. What was the original name of Canadian publishing house McClelland & Stewart?

10. This acclaimed Canadian short story writer has spent most of her adult life in Paris, France. Name her.

11. Mordecai Richler's first novel was:

    a) *Cocksure*
    b) *The Apprenticeship of Duddy Kravitz*
    c) *The Acrobats*
    d) *St. Urbain's Horseman*

12. How many Governor General's Awards has Ontario-born poet/playwright James Reaney won?

a) none
b) one
c) two
d) three
e) five

13. Which of the following authors have written for *Maclean's* magazine?

a) Pierre Berton
b) Hugh Garner
c) Peter Newman
d) Mordecai Richler
e) all of them

14. The late Milton Acorn, a native of Charlottetown, was a renowned Canadian poet. What trade was he skilled at?

a) masonry
b) plumbing
c) carpentry
d) house painting

 Answers can be found on page 69

ART FOR ART'S SAKE

- Tom Thomson's first painting, *Northern Lake*, was shown in the Ontario Society of Artists' annual exhibition in March 1913. The painting was described as "a picture full of light and vigour."

- Painting didn't come easy for Thomson. In 1914, he threw his sketch box into the woods in frustration and was so shy he could hardly be persuaded to show his sketches, which would go on to become some of Canada's most valuable paintings.

Courtesy of the National Archives of Canada, PA-125406.

Tom Thomson in Algonquin Park, where he mysteriously disappeared.

- American customs officials demanded the removal of a mural by Canadian artist Greg Curnoe being installed in Dorval Airport in Montreal in 1968 because it depicted then-president Lyndon Johnson in a plane dropping bombs. Worried about American criticism, the federal Department of Transport complied.

- When J.E.H. MacDonald's painting *The Tangled Garden* was first shown in 1916, critics thought it crude. Though it's considered an important piece today, one critic accused MacDonald, one of the original Group of Seven, of "having thrown his paint pots in the face of the public."

1. W.O. Mitchell was one of Canada's most renowned authors. What do the initials W.O. stand for?

   a) Walter Oscar
   b) Wilson Orwell
   c) William Ormond
   d) William Oliver

2. Which Canadian musician has not won a Grammy Award?

   a) Alanis Morissette
   b) Celine Dion
   c) Oscar Peterson
   d) Gordon Lightfoot

QUIZ #7

TEST YOUR ENTERTAINMENT IQ

63

3. Which of the following was not an original member of the Group of Seven?

    a) A.Y. Jackson
    b) Tom Thomson
    c) Frank Carmichael
    d) Lawren Harris

4. In 1969, John Lennon and Yoko Ono staged a famous bed-in for peace in which Canadian city?

5. Where was singer Shania Twain born?

    a) Toronto
    b) Timmins
    c) St. Catharines
    d) Windsor

6. Name the Halifax native who was the lead singer for The Mamas and the Papas.

7. Which of the following is not in the Rock and Roll Hall of Fame?

    a) Neil Young
    b) The Guess Who
    c) The Band
    d) Joni Mitchell

8. Which of the following was *not* a number one hit on the Billboard chart?

    a) "Seasons in the Sun"
    b) "Born to be Wild"
    c) "You Ain't Seen Nothing Yet"
    d) "Sundown"
    e) "Heart of Gold"

 Answers can be found on page 70

TIMELINES

January 1

1953: The National Library of Canada was established in Ottawa.

February 17

1960: The new National Gallery of Canada was opened in Ottawa by Prime Minister John Diefenbaker.

The National Gallery in 2004 in its modern-day quarters.

March 11

1930: Quebec filmmaker Claude Jutra was born in Montreal. His 1971 film *Mon Oncle Antoine* is considered by many critics to be the finest film ever made in Canada.

March 19

1914: The Royal Ontario Museum in Toronto opened its doors to the public. The ROM is one of the few museums in the world to combine art, archaeology, and science in one building.

March 23

1923: Foster Hewitt announced his first hockey game for Toronto radio station CFCA. Hewitt was known as the "voice of hockey."

April 27

1984: Harvey Kirck, well-respected longtime news announcer, delivered his final broadcast in Toronto.

May 31

1954: The first prairie television station, CBWT, went on the air in Winnipeg.

June 14

1894: Massey Hall, a new theatre in Toronto for classical music, was officially opened. The hall's acoustics were praised from the beginning, and today it remains a popular site for concerts.

The cream of the music world has played concerts at Massey Hall.

June 30

1957: The Festival Theatre at Stratford, Ontario, was officially dedicated. The theatre replaced the large canvas tent that had been home to a variety of plays at the festival since it began in 1953.

The Festival Theatre in Stratford is home to some of the best live performances in Canada.

July 8

1917: Painter Tom Thomson drowned mysteriously in Canoe Lake in Ontario's Algonquin Park.

July 13

1953: British actor Alec Guinness stepped onto the stage as Richard III in the first play performed at the Stratford Festival in Stratford, Ontario. The festival has become one of the most renowned celebrations of Shakespearean plays in the world.

July 21

1896: What is believed to be the first public exhibition of a motion picture took place in a park in Ottawa (some experts argue an earlier display occurred in Montreal). Among the films shown was *The Kiss,* with Whitby, Ontario's May Irwin.

August 28

1913: Robertson Davies, one of Canada's foremost novelists with such books as *Fifth Business* and *What's Bred in the Bone,* was born in Thamesville, Ontario.

September 6

1952: The first television program in Canada was broadcast in Montreal.

October 11

1960: The O'Keefe Centre for the Performing Arts was opened in Toronto. Today it's called the Hummingbird Centre.

November 14

1606: A play entitled Le Théâtre de Neptune en la Nouvelle-France was performed on a boat near Port Royal, Nova Scotia. It was the first play ever performed in North America.

December 1

1919: Ambrose Small, a Toronto millionaire and theatre owner, disappeared, never to be seen again. However, it's said his ghost still haunts the Grand Theatre in London, Ontario.

The Grand Theatre, said to be the home of the ghost of Ambrose Small.

December 25

1906: Reginald Aubrey Fessenden transmitted the first ever voice radio broadcast.

QUIZ ANSWERS

QUIZ #5: AN ENTERTAINING QUIZ

1. c) *Winnipeg Free Press.*

2. a) *Long Day's Journey into Night* in 1995.

3. b) The OPP. Some people mistook the letters to be OPD and thought they meant Officially Pronounced Dead, which fuelled rumours at the time that McCartney was dead.

More clues about the "Paul is dead" rumours are found on the cover of the *Sgt. Pepper* album.

4. True. He introduced them to avoid labour union problems in Hollywood.

5. e) Niagara Falls. They were taken in 1840 by Hugh Lee Pattinson, who was on a business trip.

6. c) It was Klaatu, who was subsequently named Hype of the Year in 1977 by *Rolling Stone* magazine.

7. a) The Deverons.

8. b) Seven. Shearer won most of his in the Best Sound category, while Day won for set decoration and art direction. Shearer, however, won five more plaques and citations from the Academy, and some sources credit him with twelve Oscars.

QUIZ #6:
LITERARY QUIZ

1. c) Robert W. Service appeared in the 1942 film *The Spoilers*.

2. d) Bertram Brooker won the honour for his novel *Think of the Earth*.

3. b) *The Manticore*.

4. *Pilgrim*.

5. Margaret Laurence's.

6. a) Manawaka.

7. b) *Fraggle Rock*.

8. Michael Ondaatje.

Brooker's *Think of the Earth* was the first novel to win the coveted Governor General's Award for Fiction.

9. The original name was McClelland & Goodchild, which was started in Toronto in 1906 by John McClelland and Frederick Goodchild, both former employees of the Methodist Book Room (later Ryerson Press).

Mavis Gallant spent many years in Paris.

Courtesy of the National Archives of Canada, PA-114591.

10. Mavis Gallant.

11. c) *The Acrobats*, which was published in 1954.

12. d) Three.

13. e) All of them.

14. c) Carpentry.

Courtesy of the National Archives of Canada, PA-139803.

Pierre Berton, centre, interviewing Paul Martin, Sr., during the Liberal leadership convention in 1968.

QUIZ #7:
TEST YOUR ENTERTAINMENT IQ

1. c) William Ormond.

2. d) Gordon Lightfoot has never won, although he has been nominated.

3. b) Tom Thomson.

4. Montreal.

5. d) She was born in Windsor, although she grew up in Timmins, where the Shania Twain Centre salutes her career.

The Shania Twain Museum is a popular attraction in Timmins, Ontario.

Graphic by Shania Twain Centre, Timmins, Ontario.

6. Denny Doherty.

7. b) The Guess Who.

8. b) The Canadian band Steppenwolf only reached number two with their popular rock anthem "Born to Be Wild."

NAME DROPPERS

- Timothy Eaton's first department store, which opened at Yonge and Queen streets in December 1869, was not his first retail outlet. In 1856, Timothy and his brother James opened the J. and T. Eaton General Store in Kirkton, Ontario, near Stratford.

Courtesy of the National Archives of Canada, C-14088.

Department store magnate Timothy Eaton got his start near Stratford, Ontario.

Corporate Canada is more than pinstriped suits, interest rates, takeovers, and mergers. Thanks to some inventive and interesting entrepreneurs, the world of Canadian business is chock full of quirkiness and colour, touching on everything from money, markets, and millionaires to shopping centres, sunken ships, doughnuts, the Internet, and the favourite event of generations of Canadians, the Santa Claus Parade.

- Jennie Creighton Woolworth, wife of F.W. Woolworth, founder of the famous American Woolworth's five-and-dime store chain, was born in Picton, Ontario, in 1855. Her husband, a store clerk from Watertown, New York, opened his first bargain store in 1878 and by 1911 had six hundred outlets. After F.W.'s death, Jennie Woolworth became the world's richest woman. She died on May 21, 1924.

- *Biz whizzes run in the family.* Toronto's A.E. LePage, who in the early 1900s founded the real estate company now known as Royal LePage Real Estate Services, is the nephew of William Nelson

Le Page of P.E.I., who started the LePage glue business in the early 1870s.

A.E. LePage: nephew of the glue mogul.

Courtesy of Royal LePage Real Estate Services Ltd.

• *A recipe for bad taste.* Buckley's Mixture, the Canadian-made cough syrup that tastes awful, is made from ammonium carbonate, menthol, oil of pine, and extract of Irish moss. Its inventor, Toronto pharmacist William Buckley, once referred to its taste as "brisk."

It tastes terrible but it works.

• The O-Pee-Chee company, which was famous in Canada for making such gum as Bazooka and Thrills, took its name from a line in the Longfellow poem "The Song of Hiawatha." O-Pee-Chee is a Native word meaning "robin."

• The *Accommodation* was the first all-Canadian steamship launched in Canada. The boat featured a cigar-shaped deck with a thin smokestack and was eased into the St. Lawrence River on August 19, 1809, by brewer John Molson.

- During the years the Eaton's department store chain ran Toronto's Santa Claus Parade, from 1905 to 1982, St. Nick's sleigh was always followed by a car with darkened windows carrying a doctor, a nurse, and a backup St. Nick — just in case Santa took ill.

- *Doggy-doo.* Legend has it that when Armand Bombardier invented a lightweight recreational snowmobile in 1959 in Valcourt, Quebec, he called it the Ski-Dog, but when the literature was printed, a typographical error changed the name to Ski-Doo. It stuck, and since that faux pas the company has sold more than 2 million snowmobiles worldwide.

An early version of the snowmobile.

BIZ BITES

- The first formal advertisement in Canada is believed to have been an ad to help sell butter that appeared in 1752 in the *Halifax Gazette.* But the first advertising agency didn't open until 1889, when Anson McKim created a firm in Montreal.

- In 1961, the Bank of Nova Scotia became the first Canadian bank to employ female branch managers when it appointed Shirley Giles of Toronto and Gladys Marcellus of Ottawa to the senior role.

The famous ship *Edmund Fitzgerald*, which sank in Lake Superior in November 1975, was named for the president of the Northwestern Mutual Life Insurance Company, which owned it. The ship was seventeen years old when it met its demise; it was later immortalized in a song by Gordon Lightfoot.

- The Great Depression in the 1930s was the bleakest period of Canada's economic history. By 1933 the economy had shrunk by 30 percent and the unemployment rate was 19 percent. Between 1929 and 1933, wages and salaries shrunk by 25 percent.

Riding the rails in the Depression.

Courtesy of the National Archives of Canada, C-029399.

- But then things brightened. Canadian industrial workers earned twice as much in 1941 as they had just two years earlier in 1939. The need for supplies during World War II greatly reduced the high unemployment that had existed during the Depression.

- *Start saving now.* Back in 1909, the annual tuition to obtain a Bachelor of Arts degree at the University of Toronto was just $50. In the 2003–2004 academic year, that figure had jumped to $4,107. And in 2009…?

It takes a pretty penny to pay for tuition at the University of Toronto these days.

- Until the 1960s, about 95 percent of milk consumed in Canadian homes was delivered door to door. With the advent of supermarkets and three-quart jugs, home delivery now accounts for about 1 percent of milk purchased.

- *Bottoms up.* The Liquor Control Board of Ontario (LCBO) is the largest single retailer of beverage alcohol in the world, offering more than twelve thousand products for sale through its stores, catalogue, and private ordering service from more than sixty countries. According to its latest annual report, the LCBO has more than seven hundred stores and some $3 billion in annual net sales.

Ontario, Canada's most populous province, is also the country's agricultural leader. The province produces almost 25 percent of all Canadian farm products, or more than $8 billion annually.

- Since the 1970s, canola has become a dominant crop on the Prairies; in 1998 it earned more money for farmers than wheat, the king of Canada's crops. Its current value to the Canadian economy is about $7 billion.

LCBO stores attract millions of customers each year.

- There are 102 general interest daily newspapers in Canada. The largest is the *Toronto Star*, with a circulation of about 480,000 copies each weekday, about 735,000 on Saturdays, and about 479,000 on Sundays.

- It cost two cents to mail a letter in Canada in 1910, and even by 1970 that price had only gone up to six cents. But by 2004, the price was forty-nine cents.

Family assets early in the twenty-first century in Canada, including pensions and minus all debts, average $249,000. In the late 1980s, the average family was worth $208,000.

- Truck driving is the most popular occupation for Canadian men, while the job done most by women is retail sales. Statistics Canada says about

255,900 men drive trucks, compared to 7,520 women, totalling 1.7 percent of Canada's workforce. In the retail industry, women outnumber men 355,465 to 235,600.

Keep on truckin'? **These massive vehicles are a familiar sight at truck stops along Highway 401 in Ontario.**

British Columbia is the third-largest film and television production centre in North America, after New York and Los Angeles. Early in this century, an average of more than two hundred movies and TV shows were shot in the province annually, injecting about $1 billion into the provincial economy.

- *Pondering your pension?* Registered Retirement Savings Plans may seem like a recent innovation, but Canadians have been able to contribute to the plans since 1957. Back then, about $25 million was tucked into RRSPs every year; these days Canadians invest more than $27.2 billion annually to save for retirement and shelter their savings from the taxman.

- About 24 million Canadians file tax returns every year, and 42 percent are filed electronically, says the Canada Customs and Revenue Agency.

- *Bah, humbug to Internet shopping?* Canadian shoppers spent an average of $247 online for gifts during the 2003 holiday season, totalling an estimated $972 million. This was down only slightly from 2002, when the average Canadian spent $267 online, but it's a whopping 24 percent decline from the 2001 season when they spent $324 per person on the Internet.

- *Munch on this.* Canada's snacks industry is worth about $2.7 billion in annual sales, and Canadians seem to be eating more so-called healthy snacks, says the NPD Group of Toronto. Although Canadians are eating fewer potato chips in recent years, they're snacking more on fruits, granola bars, and fat-free snacks.

1. In the early 1900s, Canada's two leading trading partners were the United States and Great Britain. What was number three?

   a) France
   b) Mexico
   c) Belgium
   d) Germany

2. In the early 1900s, J.J. McLaughlin, a member of Oshawa, Ontario's famous automobile family, made a name for himself outside of the car industry. Did he:

   a) invent and manufacture Canada Dry Ginger Ale
   b) play for the Toronto Maple Leafs
   c) represent Oshawa in the House of Commons
   d) marry an American movie star

3. Whose picture is featured on the now-defunct $1,000 bill?

4. Air Canada was the first North American airline to ban *this* from its flights in 1986. What was it?

   a) firearms in baggage
   b) metal cutlery
   c) smoking
   d) music played without headphones

5. What year did the Eaton's department store chain stop printing its popular catalogue?

   a) 1962
   b) 1968
   c) 1976
   d) 1981

6. In addition to books, which of the following product lines did Canada's Coles bookstores carry in the 1950s and 1960s?

   a) Hula Hoop and Slinky toys
   b) coffee beans
   c) pastries
   d) Polaroid cameras

QUIZ #8

A QUIZ FOR THE BIZ WHIZ

There's more to the world of business than stocks, corporate scandals, and mergers. Whether you're a senior executive, junior secretary, student of Canadian business, or a seasoned stock market player, we invite you to take a stab at our business quiz.

Jack Cole, the founder of Coles, wasn't just interested in selling books.

7. In 1929, Toronto realtor and homebuilder A.E. LePage astounded the real estate world with an amazing accomplishment. What did he do?

   a) sell every house on a downtown Toronto street in two days
   b) build a house in one day
   c) create Canada's first mobile home by converting an old streetcar into a residence
   d) sell two Toronto residences for $1 million on the same weekend

8. Twelve of the biggest fifteen oil discoveries in Canada have been in Alberta. In what two other provinces were top fifteen oil discoveries made?

9. Which of the following is not a product of Canada's early automobile industry?

   a) the Peck
   b) the Hotchkiss
   c) the Tudhope
   d) the Ivanhoe

10. What do Canadian entrepreneurs E.D. Smith, E.B. Eddy, and Frank Stanfield have in common?

    a) They all immigrated to Canada from Ireland
    b) They all played professional football
    c) They all were expelled from elementary school
    d) They all held political office

 Answers can be found on page 88

DID YOU KNOW?

• Before he established Black's Photography, Toronto businessman Eddie Black primarily sold radios. Black also sold appliances before he added to his mix the cameras and film that made him famous.

- *More to life than beer.* When Molson Breweries Ltd. launched a diversification program in 1967 its first acquisition was a furniture manufacturing firm, Vilas Industries Limited, of Cowansville, Quebec. Its second acquisition was Anthes Imperial Limited of St. Catharines, Ontario, which made pipe, steel scaffolds, furnaces, and water heaters. It later acquired Beaver Lumber and the Montreal Canadiens. In a bid to return to its roots, Molson has since sold each of these assets, although it continues to own a 20 percent share in the Canadiens.

- Alphonse Desjardins of Quebec introduced the idea of credit unions to North America when he established the first such co-operative institution in Levis, Quebec, in 1900. He later helped spread the idea to the rest of Canada and the U.S. Today there are more than 70 million credit union members in the two countries.

> Labour Day parades were held in Canada for about ten years before Americans adopted the practice. Parades and rallies took place in Ottawa and Toronto in 1872, while the first American festivities didn't take place until 1882. The official Labour Day holiday was established in Canada in 1894.

© Canada Post Corporation, 1975. Reproduced with permission.

Alphonse Desjardins, father of credit unions.

A typical credit union in Canada.

- When the first old-age pension was introduced in Canada in 1927, it paid up to $20 a month depending on a person's other income and assets. The pension was available to British subjects seventy years and older with twenty years of residence in Canada.

- The 340-foot-long bar at Lulu's Roadhouse in Kitchener, Ontario, was once in the *Guinness Book*

Bean there, done that. In 1998, Canada surpassed Turkey as the world's largest exporter of lentils. Alberta, Manitoba, and Saskatchewan are the prime growers of this plant, which wasn't even produced in Canada until the mid-1960s.

of World Records as the longest on the planet. But it was cut in two in the 1990s, and the record now goes to a bar 405 feet, 10 inches long in South Bass Island, Ohio.

- Fifty years ago the tallest building in Canada was the Bank of Commerce in Toronto, rising 34 storeys to 145 metres. In the early twenty-first century that building wouldn't even make it into the top ten tallest Canadian office towers.

- In 1992 London, Ontario, lawyer Julius Melnitzer pleaded guilty to defrauding a handful of Canadian banks, friends, and business associates of a whopping $67 million. Among his victims was the Canadian Imperial Bank of Commerce, which was burned for $8.4 million.

- In Canada, 60 percent of households own their home, while about one-third have mortgages. The average outstanding mortgage is $76,000.

- Approximately 11 million used tires are generated in Ontario each year. As many as 5 million are recycled and used for such things as automotive parts, playground and sports surfaces, running tracks, loading dock bumpers, and mats.

Worn-out tires have a multitude of uses.

- Foreign-controlled companies are very successful at attracting and signing established Canadian musical talent. Although these firms reported only 20 percent of the new releases by Canadian artists, they accumulated 49 percent of the net sales by Canadian singers and bands.

1. In 1895, the treasurer of which country proposed free trade with Canada?

   a) Australia
   b) Great Britain
   c) France
   d) New Zealand
   e) Iceland

2. June 1967 was an important time in Canadian banking because:

   a) banks were authorized to make residential mortgage loans
   b) Canada went off the gold standard
   c) the Bank of Canada was founded
   d) the federal government removed the 6 percent ceiling on interest rates charged by banks

3. Where was the first drive-in restaurant in Canada?

   a) Toronto
   b) Halifax
   c) Vancouver
   d) Windsor
   e) Brandon

4. CCM, once an automobile manufacturer, is the world's leading maker of hockey equipment. What do the initials CCM stand for?

   a) Canada Cycle and Motor Company
   b) Canadian Car Manufacturing Limited
   c) Cycles Cars and Motors Limited

CCM hockey equipment is known around the world.

5. What do the initials "V.O." stand for in Seagram's V.O. whisky?

   a) Very Own
   b) Vapour Oxidized
   c) Very Old
   d) Vital Osmosis

Canada's V.O. whisky.

6. Who said the U.S. "got screwed by Canada" when the Canada–U.S. Autopact was signed in 1965 to remove duties on trucks, cars, and auto parts moving between Canada and the U.S.?

   a) Canadian Labour Leader Bob White
   b) U.S. President Lyndon Johnson
   c) automaker Henry Ford, Jr.
   d) Lee Iacocca, former president of Chrysler

7. The first recorded distillery in Canada was set up in what city in 1769?

   a) Quebec City
   b) Montreal
   c) Halifax
   d) Saint John
   e) Summerside

8. Where was Canada's first significant oil industry based?

   a) Turner Valley, Alberta
   b) Oil Springs, Ontario
   c) Red Bay, Labrador
   d) Cutknife, Saskatchewan

9. What was hockey player and budding doughnut magnate Tim Horton's first business venture?

   a) a service station and car dealership
   b) a hockey school
   c) a chain of pizza outlets
   d) a men's clothing store

Doughnuts weren't Tim Horton's first business.

10. Who is the elderly character pictured on Canadian Tire money?

    a)   Sandy McTire
    b)   Scotty Canadian
    c)   Douglas MacAuto
    d)   Thomas O'Tool

Canadian Tire stores are a familiar fixture in many Canadian communities.

 Answers can be found on page 89

MONEY, MONEY, MONEY

- *A pioneering kind of credit card.* When French troops in Canada became mutinous in 1685 for not being paid, officials issued them playing cards with a monetary value written on the back. This practice existed until 1717.

- In 1922, Canada's Royal Mint (later the Royal Canadian Mint) replaced the inconvenient small, silver five-cent piece with a coin made from nickel. To no one's surprise, these soon became known as "nickels."

- The first financial institution in Canada to have an operational automated banking machine

Phony as a four-dollar bill? The last Dominion of Canada four-dollar notes were issued in 1911. They were replaced in 1912 by Dominion of Canada five-dollar notes.

The Royal Canadian Mint: not just any nickel and dime operation.

83

was the Sherwood Credit Union in Regina. The
year: 1977.

- The best-known photo taken by the late photographer Malak Karsh of Ottawa depicts logs and a tug-
boat named the *Missinaibi* floating along the
Ottawa River against the backdrop of the
Parliament Buildings. It appeared on the back of
3.4 billion Canadian one-dollar bills printed
between 1973 and 1989. The boat is on display at
the Museum of Civilization in Gatineau, Quebec.

- The Bank of Canada issued the last one-dollar bills
in 1989, and in 1996 the bank withdrew the two-
dollar note. The bills were replaced by one-dollar
coins known as "loonies" and two-dollar coins
named "twonies."

**Loonies and twonies
have replaced $1
and $2 bills.**

- On the tails side of the one-dollar coin, you'll find
the letters RRC. They are the initials of the man
who designed the loonie, Robert Ralph Carmichael.

- At the beginning of the twentieth century, Canada's
largest bank was the Canadian Bank of Commerce
in terms of total assets. And the biggest at the
beginning of the twenty-first century? The
Canadian Imperial Bank of Commerce. By 2003,
however, it was number two behind the Royal Bank
of Canada.

TIMELINES

January 1

1985: Nancy Eaton, great-great-granddaughter of department store tycoon Timothy Eaton, was found dead in her Toronto apartment, a victim of multiple stab wounds.

January 4

1817: The first stagecoach service began between York (now Toronto) and Kingston, Ontario. The fare was equivalent to eighteen dollars.

February 11

1901: The first annual report of the federal Bureau of Labour deplored the continued employment of children under twelve.

February 25

1972: Ontario Hydro's Pickering nuclear power plant opened, becoming the largest single producer of electricity in the world.

Courtesy of Ontario Power Generation.

An aerial view of the Pickering nuclear power plant near Toronto.

March 2

1943: Eleven Ontario real estate boards and delegates from Victoria, Vancouver, Edmonton, Winnipeg, and Montreal drew up the first constitution of the Canadian Association of Real Estate Boards (CAREB), forerunner to the Canadian Real Estate Association.

March 19

1997: Michael de Guzman, a geologist with Bre-X Minerals Ltd. of Calgary, died after jumping out of a helicopter over Borneo. Seven weeks later, the world was shocked to discover de Guzman was part of a swindle that had faked the biggest gold-mining discovery in history in Indonesia.

April 10	**1912:** The board of Grain Commissioners was appointed to supervise grain inspection and regulate trade.
April 16	**1903:** Canada raised the tariff on goods imported from Germany in retaliation to a similar move by Germany.
April 18	**1872:** A bill calling for the legalization of trade unions was introduced in Parliament.
May 14	**1968:** The fifty-six-storey Toronto-Dominion Centre in Toronto opened. At the time, it was the tallest building in Canada.
June 22	**1774:** English-speaking merchants expressed outrage with the passing of the Quebec Act, which reaffirmed freedom of worship for Roman Catholics and provided for the use of French-style government and civil law.
June 28	**1968:** The 190-metre (626-foot) Husky Tower in Calgary opened. Since renamed the Calgary Tower, it has often been referred to as the baby CN Tower.
July 6	**1906:** Parliament passed the Lord Day's Act, which forbade working on Sundays and most Sunday transportation. Seventy-nine years later the Supreme Court ruled the Act unconstitutional.
July 19	**1852:** Charles Woodward, founder of the Woodward chain of department stores, was born in Hamilton, Ontario. He opened his first store in Vancouver in 1891.
August 17	**1904:** The Ford Motor Company of Canada was incorporated, with production beginning on October 10 at Walkerville, Ontario. The company produced 117 cars in its first year.

Courtesy of Ford of Canada Archives.

Ford's first Canadian auto production plant.

September 3	**1962:** The Trans-Canada Highway, one of the biggest construction projects in Canadian history, was opened.
September 12	**1945:** A strike against Ford began in Windsor that would ultimately lead to the introduction of the Rand Formula that provided for better union security.
September 23	**1985:** John Fraser resigned as Fisheries Minister after releasing more than 1 million cans of tuna that were declared unfit for human consumption.
October 2	**1912:** The world's largest grain elevator opened in Montreal. It was capable of holding 2.5 million bushels, equal to the combined capacity of all the other elevators in Montreal's port at the time.
October 10	**1958:** The last weld was completed on the Trans-Canada Pipeline. It took twenty-eight months to build the 2,290-kilometre line that ran from Burstall, Saskatchewan, to Kapuskasing, Ontario.
October 19	**1987:** "Black Monday" brought about the greatest drop in share prices in the history of the Toronto Stock Exchange and the New York Stock Exchange.
November 6	**1958:** North America's deepest coalmine collapsed at Springfield, Nova Scotia, trapping 174 miners. Seventy-five died.
November 22	**1957:** The first ship passed through the Iroquois Lock, the first lock of the St. Lawrence Seaway to be completed.
December 8	**1919:** A bronze statue of Timothy Eaton was erected at Eaton's Queen Street store in Toronto to celebrate the fiftieth anniversary of the department store chain founded by Timothy Eaton. Over the years passersby wore the toe of the left shoe shiny by rubbing it in hopes of obtaining some of Timothy's good fortune.

QUIZ ANSWERS

QUIZ #8:
A QUIZ FOR THE BIZ WHIZ

1. d) Germany, but a few years later France pushed it to number four.

2. a) J.J. McLaughlin, a pharmacist, invented and manufactured Canada Dry Ginger Ale.

Canada Dry was a druggist's creation.

3. Queen Elizabeth's. She was also on the old one and two dollar bills, and is currently on the $20 bill.

Queen Elizabeth's portrait is still on Canadian $20 bills.

4. c) Smoking. Fifteen years earlier, the carrier had introduced no-smoking sections in its aircraft.

5. c) 1976. The catalogue had been a mainstay in Canadian homes since 1884.

6. a) The Hula Hoop and the Slinky were sold as part of Coles' sporting goods and toys lineup.

7. b) LePage built a five-bedroom house in Toronto in twenty-four hours.

8. Major discoveries were also made in Newfoundland and Saskatchewan.

9. b) The Hotchkiss, which was manufactured in France beginning in 1912.

10. d) They all held political office: E.D. Smith, founder of E.D. Smith & Sons Ltd., was an Ontario MP and senator; E.B. Eddy, founder of Eddy Match Company (later E.B. Eddy Ltd.) was a member of the Quebec Legislative Assembly and mayor of Hull, Quebec; Stanfield, son of Charles Stanfield, founder of Stanfield's Ltd., an underwear and apparel maker, was an MLA in Nova Scotia.

QUIZ #9:
BIZ QUIZ II

1. d) New Zealand.

2. d) Removal of the 6 percent ceiling on interest rates charged by banks.

3. c) Canada's first drive-in restaurant was opened in Vancouver in 1928 by Nat Bailey, a native of St. Paul, Minnesota. The outlet, which was famous for its carhops and barbecued sandwiches, evolved into the White Spot restaurant chain.

4. a) Canada Cycle and Motor Company.

5. a) Very Own. The whisky was a special blend that Joseph Seagram developed to celebrate his son Thomas's wedding.

6. b) Lyndon Johnson, in a conversation with Canadian ambassador Charles Ritchie.

7. a) Quebec City. It was used to make rum from imported molasses.

8. c) Red Bay, Labrador, where in the sixteenth century a full-blown whale oil industry existed off the coast of Labrador for about five generations.

9. a) A service station and car dealership.

10. a) Sandy McTire has been a featured character on Canadian Tire money since 1958.

CHAPTER FOUR

COLOUR-FUL CANUCKS

Canadians have made their mark in many different fields and endeavours. Some have been innovators, while others have become famous simply for their persistence, hard work, and dedication. Meet some Canadians who have either changed our lives or made them more interesting.

INNOVATION, CANADIAN STYLE

- John B. Maclean, the founder of *Maclean's* magazine, started his journalism career only after he failed to qualify for a job as a high-school principal. He didn't get the principal's post because his marks in English weren't high enough.

- The Jolly Jumper, which has kept youngsters everywhere happy and healthy, was invented in British Columbia in 1959 by Olivia Poole, who is originally from the White Earth Reservation in Minnesota. About one in every five Canadian babies uses the device.

- Dr. James Gosling, who grew up near Calgary, developed Java, a universal computer programming language. Originally known as Oak, it can be used with platforms such as Unix and Windows.

- Adelaide Hunter Hoodless of St. George, near Brantford, Ontario, helped establish the Victorian Order of Nurses, Women's Institutes, the National Council of Women of Canada, the National Council of the YWCA, the Macdonald Institute in Ontario, and Macdonald College in Quebec. She was motivated to help women take good care of their children after one of her children, an infant son, died in 1889 after drinking infected milk.

- Dr. Wilbur Franks of Weston, Ontario, developed the anti-gravity suit, the G-suit for short, in the late 1930s and early 1940s. It allowed fighter pilots

Dr. Wilbur Franks.

Courtesy of the National Archives of Canada, PA-63866.

to carry out high-speed, high-altitude manoeuvres without blacking out and was the precursor to modern-day astronaut suits.

- Kit Coleman, who wrote for the *Toronto Mail*, became the world's first accredited female war correspondent when she travelled to Cuba and reported on the Spanish-American War in the late 1800s.

- Toronto native Dr. Elliott Jacques coined the term "midlife crisis" in 1965 after his research showed abrupt changes in style or declines in productivity among artists and composers around the age of thirty-five. Jacques died in March 2003.

- Canadian Isabelle Budd invented the double breast prosthesis, a camisole with pockets for removable pads, for women who have lost their breasts to cancer and other ailments or injuries. Where others were heavy and uncomfortable, Budd's was lightweight and easy to wear. She created the prosthesis after her own double mastectomy and applied for a patent in 1986.

- *One cool customer.* Henry Ruttan of Cobourg, Ontario, introduced air conditioning to train travel in 1858 by channelling a flow of air through a ventilating cap and over a shallow coldwater tank placed on top of a rail car.

> "The Real McCoy," a phrase common today, is credited by some sources to Elijah McCoy, a black Canadian from Colchester, Ontario, who created a self-lubricating cup that kept machines oiled. His invention was in such demand that those who had it boasted about having "the Real McCoy." Other sources say the term comes from the nickname of an American boxer or from a scotch whisky that was known as the "Real MacKay."

> The first woman to attend a University of Toronto lecture was Catherine Brown, youngest daughter of George Brown, founder of *The Globe* newspaper and a prominent politician. Catherine and her older sister Margaret were among the University of Toronto's first five women graduates in 1885. Both received bachelor of arts degrees in modern languages.

- Anna Sutherland Bissell, a native of River John, Nova Scotia, helped design, build, and market the Bissell carpet sweeper that would become a friend to homeowners everywhere. Bissell and her husband, Melville, patented the sweeper in 1876 in Grand Rapids, Michigan, where she often became frustrated when sawdust became embedded in the carpet of her crockery shop.

- Sir Sandford Fleming, a civil engineer who immigrated to Canada from Scotland in 1845, is well known for overseeing major surveys when Canada's transcontinental railway was built in the late 1800s. In addition, he designed the "Three-Penny Beaver," Canada's first adhesive postage stamp, and a pair of in-line skates, and proposed the present system of standard time, which in 1884 divided the world into twenty-four equal time zones.

Canada's first adhesive postage stamp.

© Canada Post Corporation, 1851. Reproduced with permission.

- In 1902, Sir Ernest Rutherford, then a physics professor at McGill University in Montreal, sent what was reputedly the world's first wireless telegraph message from a moving train while on board the Grand Trunk's International Limited as it raced from Toronto to Montreal.

Although Ottawa's Charlotte Whitton gained fame in 1951 as the first female mayor of a major Canadian city, she wasn't the first woman to sit on a municipal council. That honour goes to Mary Teresa Sullivan, who was sworn in as a Halifax city councillor in 1936.

- Earle Kelly, a *Vancouver Province* reporter known as "Mr. Good Evening," was Canada's first personality newscaster. Over a period of twenty years beginning in the early 1920s, his nightly fifteen-minute summaries were heard on Vancouver stations CKCD, CNRV, and CKWX. Kelly was remembered for his sign-off, wishing viewers "a restful good evening."

- Chemistry professor Thomas Sterry Hunt of McGill University in Montreal came up with the ink the United States chose to print its money with, beginning in 1862. The special green ink couldn't be reproduced by photography, making it nearly impossible for forgers to produce phony "greenbacks."

Courtesy of University of Toronto Archives.

- In 1920, Annie Laird and Clara Benson earned groundbreaking titles by becoming the first female professors at the University of Toronto — thirty-six years after women were first admitted to the university.

Courtesy of University of Toronto Archives.

Annie Laird and Clara Benson broke ground at U of T.

- As the publisher and editor of the *Provincial Freeman*, a black newspaper in Chatham, Ontario, from 1853 until 1859, Mary Ann Shadd was the first black woman to be an editor in North America. She was also a respected educator and abolitionist.

---

1. Name the Ottawa photographer who gained world-wide fame with his portraits of such well-known figures as Winston Churchill, Ernest Hemingway, and Albert Einstein.

2. Of these three explorers, who first reached what is now Canada — Samuel de Champlain, John Cabot, or Jacques Cartier?

3. True or false? A Canadian invented the Wonderbra in 1964.

4. What was Terry Fox's run across Canada in 1980 better known as?

5. What is Winnie Roach Leuszler's claim to fame?

   a) first Canadian woman pilot

QUIZ #10

QUIZZING CANADIANS

Test your knowledge about some exceptional Canucks.

b) first Canadian world champion in her sport
c) first Canadian woman to swim the English Channel
d) first Canadian woman to scale Mount Everest

6. Thomas Wilby and F.V. Haney gained fame in 1912 for *this*:

   a) first Canadians to appear on radio
   b) first to drive across Canada
   c) first to fly in a helicopter
   d) first two Members of Parliament to receive a government pension

7. In May 1877, this great Sioux chief crossed into Canada with hundreds of his people and thousands of horses seeking a safe haven from the Americans after the Battle of the Little Bighorn. Name him.

8. What was Marshall McLuhan's first name?

   a) Joseph
   b) Herbert
   c) Marshall
   d) Peter

9. About 125 libraries were built in Canada from 1901 to 1923 because of grants from a wealthy American. Who was it?

   a) Henry Ford
   b) Andrew Carnegie
   c) J. P. Morgan
   d) John Rockefeller

10. True or false? Canadian cartoonist Lynn Johnston, known for her strip *For Better or Worse,* began her career illustrating medical journals.

 Answers can be found on page 106

WHO WOULD HAVE GUESSED?

- Before becoming a political leader in the 1860s, famous Canadian rebel leader Louis Riel trained for the priesthood and worked as a law clerk in Montreal.

- When Robert Simpson, the founder of the old Simpson's department stores, died in 1897, his biggest rival, Timothy Eaton, attended the funeral, and all of Eaton's stores flew their flags at half-mast that day.

- Charles Edward Saunders, best remembered as the man who developed Marquis wheat, a strain that could be grown in Canada's cold climate, was a reluctant chemist. Saunders wanted to study flute with a celebrated teacher in Germany, but his father convinced him to study chemistry instead.

> In a 1940 speech, Adolf Hitler said Canada's low population density made it an easy country to run. Said the Führer: "No matter how stupidly one managed one's affairs in such a country, a decent living would still be possible."

> Harry Houdini, famous escape artist, died in 1926 of peritonitis brought on by a ruptured appendix several days after being punched in the stomach by McGill University student Joceyln Gordon Whitehead. Though some blamed Whitehead for the great magician's death, medical experts today say the punch wasn't a factor.

- Joseph Burr Tyrrell, the geologist and explorer who discovered the rich dinosaur beds of southern Alberta, developed his love for exploration as a youngster while collecting mud turtles, crayfish, and grasshoppers near his family's farm in the Humber Valley near Toronto.

Joseph Tyrrell loved to collect turtles.

Courtesy of the National Archives of Canada, C-081838.

Anna Leonowens, whose life inspired the Broadway musical and film *The King and I* and the more recent film *Anna and the King,* lived for about thirty-five years in Canada. While living in Halifax she helped found the Halifax Council of Women and the Victoria School of Art and Design, which later became the Nova Scotia College of Art and Design. She died in Montreal in 1915.

One of novelist Charles Dickens's sons, Francis Jeffrey, served in Canada with the Northwest Mounted Police for several years until 1886. His career was once described as "unspectacular."

- Though Stephen Leacock is best known for his humorous writings in such books as *Sunshine Sketches of a Little Town,* he was also an economics and political science professor at McGill University in Montreal. *Elements of Political Science* was his best-selling book during his lifetime.

- Gabriel Dumont, a Metis leader who fought alongside Louis Riel in the 1885 Rebellion, later escaped to the U.S. and became a performer in Buffalo Bill's Wild West Show. Eventually he was granted amnesty by the government and returned to Canada.

Gabriel Dumont went into showbiz.

Courtesy of the National Archives of Canada, C-27663.

- Canadian Lloyd Shirley was the producer behind such British TV shows as *Rumpole of the Bailey, The Sweeney,* and *The Rivals of Sherlock Holmes.* The London, Ontario, native worked in TV in Canada before heading to Britain in the 1950s, where he established his name as one of the best in the business. He died in March 2003.

- Canada has two patron saints, Joseph, the spouse of the Virgin Mary, and Ann, who was Mary's mother. Joseph is also patron saint to carpenters and the countries of China and Belgium, while Anne is also the saint of housewives and women in labour.

- *Mr. Versatility.* Gene Lockhart of London, Ontario, was best known as an Oscar-nominated Hollywood actor in the 1930s and '40s. But before that he won the mile-long swimming championship of Canada in 1909, played football with the Toronto Argonauts, acted on Broadway and on radio, and wrote a major hit song, "The World Is Waiting for the Sunrise."

- Sir George Yonge, for whom Toronto's Yonge Street is named, never visited Canada. Born in England in 1731, Yonge was a British MP and master of the mint. The street was named for him by his good friend John Graves Simcoe, the lieutenant-governor of Upper Canada.

Toronto's Yonge Street remains one of the most famous avenues in the country.

- Lord Stanley of Preston, governor general of Canada from 1888 to 1893, donated the trophy that is given annually to the National Hockey League's championship team. But he never saw a Stanley Cup playoff game or presentation of the trophy because he returned to England when his term as governor general was up.

- When Canadian ballerina Evelyn Hart was eleven years old, she was rejected by the National Ballet School, which said she didn't have a dancer's body. In 1973, six years later, she was a member of the Royal Winnipeg Ballet and was dancing major roles in ballets such as *The Nutcracker* and *Sleeping Beauty*. Eventually, she was awarded the Order of Canada.

- Nathan Cohen, a pioneering Canadian theatre critic in the middle of the twentieth century, got his start in journalism editing a mine union newspaper in Glace Bay, Nova Scotia. He also wrote for communist newspapers in Toronto before turning his attention to reviewing plays.

ODDS AND ENDS

Chicago mobster Al Capone once replied, "I don't even know what street Canada is on" when asked if our country was the main source of supply for his lucrative bootlegging operations in the 1920s. Capone later spent time in Alcatraz prison.

- Harriet Tubman of St. Catharines, Ontario, who was known as the "Black Moses," travelled deep into U.S. slave states to help lead more than three hundred slaves out of bondage, even though she had a $40,000 bounty on her head.

- Diamond Tooth Gertie's, Canada's first legal gambling hall, bar, and cancan show palace, opened in 1971 in Dawson City in the Yukon Territory. It was named for Gertie Lovejoy, who worked in Dawson's dance halls during the gold rush era in the late 1890s and wore a small diamond between two of her teeth.

- Long before Ken Taylor helped spirit American hostages out of Iran in 1980, another Canadian pulled off a similar feat near the Black Sea. Just after the Russian Revolution of 1917, Joe Boyle of Woodstock, Ontario, helped more than seventy Romanian hostages escape from their Bolshevik guards at the port of Theodosia and return to their homeland.

Emily Carr, who died in 1945, is renowned across Canada for her paintings of Native villages in British Columbia. But she also won the Governor General's Award for Non-Fiction in 1941 for her book *Klee Wyck*.

- New Brunswick financier Max Aitken is known as Lord Beaverbrook, but long before King George V gave him the title, he was known as the "merger king." Aitken founded Canada Cement in 1909 from eleven smaller cement companies in Alberta, Ontario, and Quebec, and the next year he founded the Steel Company of Canada, better known as Stelco. He was a newspaper baron and a strong supporter of universities and the arts.

- *Mike the pilot.* Former prime minister Lester B. Pearson was known as Mike to his friends. He got the nickname from his World War I flying instructor, who didn't think Lester was a good name for a pilot.

- Although Frederick Banting and Charles Best were considered co-discovers of insulin, only Banting was awarded the Nobel Prize for medicine in 1923. He shared his winnings with Best, though.

> Norma Macmillan of Vancouver was the voice of Casper the Friendly Ghost. Macmillan, who died in March 2001, was also the voice of several other cartoon characters, including the bendable green Gumby and Sweet Polly Purebred in the Underdog TV cartoon series.

- Between 1941 and 1947, Hal Rogers, founder of Canada's Kinsmen Club (now known as Kin Canada), raised about $3 million and sent more than 50 million quarts of milk, in powdered form, to help millions of British children battle malnutrition during and after World War II.

Courtesy of Diane Rogers.

Kinsman Hal Rogers was a fundraiser.

- Alvin "Old Creepy" Karpis, a Montreal-born bank robber and kidnapper, holds the dubious honour of serving the most prison time on Alcatraz Island — twenty-six years. Karpis gained his notoriety as a henchman for the famous Barker Gang and was public enemy number one in the mid-1930s before his arrest.

- Horace Greeley, nephew of the famed American newspaper editor of the same name, didn't head west as his uncle had urged young men to do in the 1800s. Instead, the younger Greeley came north to Canada's Prairies, where he made his living first as a rancher and later as a member of the legislature.

- Canada wasn't the only country traversed by Steve Fonyo, the one-legged athlete who ran across this nation in 1984–85 to raise money for cancer research. Steve also ran from the northern tip of Great Britain to the southern tip in 1987 to raise research funds.

MORE CANADIAN FIRSTS AND FOREMOSTS

- In 1793, Alexander Mackenzie, an explorer and fur trader who was raised in Montreal, became the first white person north of Mexico to reach the Pacific Ocean by taking an overland route.

A bright idea. Henry Woodward and Matthew Evans of Toronto produced the first light bulb a good six years before Thomas Edison. The famed American inventor actually bought the rights to the Torontonians' patent. They had been unsuccessful in exploiting their invention because potential investors believed the idea would be too costly.

- Daniel David Palmer of Port Perry, Ontario, is considered to be the world's first chiropractor. While working in Iowa in 1865, Palmer supposedly cured a man of hearing loss by straightening his spine. He began to study how manipulation of the spine solves health problems and later taught his techniques to others.

- John Ware, who was born as a slave in the southern United States, moved with his family to Alberta (then part of the Northwest Territories) from Texas in 1882. Ware is credited with bringing longhorn cattle to Canada and with developing the rodeo in Canada's west.

- Anyone frustrated by slot-head screwdrivers that slip out of the screws can thank Peter Lymburner Robertson for inventing the square-head screws and

Robertson screwdrivers that can be used instead. He came up with the idea in Milton, Ontario, in 1908, turned down Henry Ford's offer to buy the patent rights, and died a millionaire forty-three years later.

Robertson screwdrivers are found in many Canadian households.

• Judson Pulford Henderson is known as the father of Canada's radio time service. In the 1920s, while working at the Dominion Observatory in Ottawa, he built a transmitter that broadcast the correct time over short-wave radio airwaves from a station operated by the observatory and later the Ottawa-based National Research Council. Known as the Dominion Time Signal, it was first broadcast in 1929 and is Canada's longest running radio show. Since November 5, 1939, it has also been heard on CBC Radio at 12:59 p.m. and Radio Canada at 11:59 a.m.

William Leonard Hunt was known in the 1800s as The Great Farini. In addition to his thrilling high-wire acts, the Port Hope, Ontario-born daredevil masterminded the first human cannonball act and invented folding theatre seats and the modern parachute.

• Dr. Maude Abbott, a member of the Canadian Medical Hall of Fame and considered a worldwide pioneer in laying the foundation for modern heart surgery in the early twentieth century, was never promoted higher than assistant professor at McGill University in Montreal.

Heart surgeon Dr. Maude Abbott never scored a big promotion.

© Canada Post Corporation, 1999–2000. Reproduced with permission.

The idea of having white lines down the middle of highways is thought to have originated near the Ontario-Quebec border in 1930. J.D. Millar is credited with introducing the lines; his boss at the Ministry of Transportation thought the innovation was foolish.

- Elsie Gregory MacGill was Canada's first female electrical engineer, the only woman in the world to hold a graduate degree in aeronautical engineering in the early 1930s, and the first woman to become a corporate member of the Engineering Institute of Canada.

- Winnipeg native John Hopps invented the pacemaker in a National Research Council laboratory in 1950 to keep the weak of heart alive and kicking.

- James Gladstone was Canada's first Native senator. A member of the Blood tribe, Gladstone was appointed to the Senate in February 1958 and gave his first speech there in Blackfoot.

- *A bloody good drink.* In 1969 when Walter Chell was working at the Westin Hotel in Calgary, he developed the Bloody Caesar. Made with vodka, Clamato juice, Worcester sauce, salt and pepper, and garnished with a celery stalk, the drink has become a favourite at bars, brunches, and backyard barbecues.

GOOD TO THE LAST SPOONFUL

- Pablum, the vitamin-enriched ready-to-use baby food that came onto the Canadian market in 1931, wasn't the first nutritional breakthrough for Drs. Frederick

The cereal that babies loved.

Courtesy of the Hospital for Sick Children.

Tisdall and Theodore Drake, who invented the cereal at the Hospital for Sick Children in Toronto. In early 1930, they developed the Sunwheat "irradiated" biscuit, which contained whole wheat, wheat germ, milk, butter, yeast, bone meal, iron, and copper and was high in several vitamins.

- More than $1 million in royalties from the sale of Pablum and Sunwheat biscuits helped establish the Sick Kids Research Institute, and over the years the money has contributed to key medical breakthroughs such as the discovery of the cystic fibrosis gene and the surgical correction for the heart defect that causes "blue babies."

- The name "Pablum" is derived from the Latin "pabulum," meaning food. The cereal, which was immediately glommed down by babies when it was introduced in 1931, is a mixture of wheatmeal, oatmeal, cornmeal, wheat germ, brewer's yeast, bone meal, and alfalfa. Media reports at the time said the cereal tasted like "boiled Kleenex" and "had the consistency of mucilage and smelled like the inside of an old cardboard box."

TIMELINES

January 9

1868: Irene Parlby, a women's rights leader, was born in London, England. She later served in the Alberta legislature and became the second women in the British Commonwealth to hold a cabinet position.

February 4

1880: In one of the most notorious murders in Canadian history, five members of the Donnelly family were massacred in Biddulph Township, near Lucan, Ontario. No one was convicted.

The Donnelly tombstone in Lucan, Ontario, provides details on some of the murdered family members.

February 23

1909: John Alexander Douglas McCurdy flew the Alexander Graham Bell-designed aircraft, the *Silver Dart,* at Baddeck, Nova Scotia. It was the first powered flight in Canada or the British Empire.

Courtesy of the National Archives of Canada, PA-89117.

John McCurdy, right, was Canada's aircraft pioneer.

March 9

1967: Gordon Hamilton Southam was appointed the first director of the National Arts Centre in Ottawa.

March 13

1928: Eileen Volick became the first Canadian woman to earn her pilot's licence. She also became the first female pilot to fly a ski-plane.

April 22

1844: William Harris founded the *Bytown Packet,* which later became the *Ottawa Citizen.*

May 3

1915: John McCrae of Guelph, Ontario, wrote "In Flanders Fields" during World War I. It was composed in Ypres, first published in December 1915, and is recited annually at Remembrance Day ceremonies.

May 8

1842: Michael Power was consecrated the first Roman Catholic bishop of Toronto.

May 24

1912: Charles Saunders made the first parachute jump in Canada in Vancouver.

May 31

1968: Dr. Pierre Grondin of the Montreal Heart Institute performed Canada's first heart transplant.

June 8

1824: The first patent issued in what would become Canada went to Noah Cushing of Quebec for a washing and fulling machine.

July 7	**1787:** Frances Barkley, married to Charles Barkley, captain of the *Imperial Beagle*, became the first white woman to arrive in British Columbia.
July 10	**1960:** Roger Woodward, age seven, became the first person to accidentally fall over Niagara's Horseshoe Falls and live.
July 31	**1913:** Alys Bryant was the first woman in Canada to make a solo airplane flight. She took off from a Vancouver racetrack.
August 3	**1751:** The first printing press in Canada was established at Halifax by Bartholomew Green.
August 8	**1863:** Angus McAskill, the Giant of Cape Breton, died. He was seven feet, nine inches tall and weighed about 400 pounds (180 kilograms).
September 16	**1901:** The Duke and Duchess of Cornwall, later to become King George V and Queen Mary, started their visit to Canada. They stayed until October 21.
October 27	**1918:** World War I airman William Barker of Manitoba destroyed four German aircraft in the skies over France, an achievement that earned him the Victoria Cross.
November 13	**1938:** Canadian surgeon Dr. Norman Bethune, who first gained fame for his medical work in the Spanish Civil War, died in China while treating the wounded during an invasion by Japan.
December 11	**1962:** The last judicial hanging in Canada took place in Toronto's Don Jail when Ronald Turpin and Arthur Lucas were executed for murder.

QUIZ ANSWERS

QUIZ #10: QUIZZING CANADIANS

1. Yousuf Karsh.

2. Cabot did, in 1497 (Cartier arrived in 1534, de Champlain in 1603).

3. True. It was invented by Louise Poirier.

4. The Marathon of Hope.

5. c) She was the first Canadian woman to swim the English Channel.

6. b) They were the first to drive across Canada. Although some parts of the country didn't even have roads then, the two made the trip in fifty-two days.

7. Sitting Bull.

8. b) Herbert.

9. b) Carnegie.

10. True.

Courtesy of the Sun Media Corp.

Terry Fox's cross-Canada marathon ended near Thunder Bay, Ontario, when his cancer returned.

A LITTLE BIT OF THIS, A LITTLE BIT OF THAT

- The original McIntosh apple tree was discovered at Dundela, in southeastern Ontario, in 1811 by farmer John McIntosh. It bore fruit until 1908 and died in 1910, shortly after being burnt in a fire.

  A monument near where the first McIntosh apple tree once grew.

  Photo by Marcus Ray.

- The Spartan apple, introduced in the 1930s, was the result of research by Dr. R.C. Palmer, director of the Summerland Experimental Station in British Columbia. The apple is said to be a cross between a McIntosh and Newtown, but Agriculture Canada says recent DNA testing shows the Newtown wasn't involved. Spartans are the third most widely grown apple in B.C.

- There are several thousand species of moths in Canada. The cecropia moth is the country's largest, with a wingspan of about twelve centimetres.

- *Heavy reading.* A hundred-page Canadian newspaper contains an average of more than three hundred thousand words of reading material, equivalent to three full-length novels.

  Words, words, and more words.

CHAPTER FIVE

ODDS AND SODS

It's time to tantalize your taste for trivia with a collection of weird and wacky items that touch on events, people, places, and daily happenings that don't fit neatly into other chapters. Here you'll find everything from the origins of Canada's most famous apple and the site of Canada's first automobile accident to how much television Canadians watch and the site of Canada's oldest golf course.

- The average height of Canadian women is 163 centimetres, or 5 feet, 4 inches. Their average weight is 65.8 kilograms, or 145 pounds. The average height of Canadian men is 178 centimeters, or 5 feet, 10 inches. Their average weight is 83.2 kilograms, or 183 pounds.

- Yes, Canadians have earned more than Americans. In 1976, the average annual income earned by a Canadian family was $15,000, slightly more than that of the median American family. It was the only time, to date, that average Canadian family incomes have been higher than those of American households.

Dr. Perry Doolittle

Dr. Perry Doolittle, a native of Elgin County in southwestern Ontario, founded the Canadian Automobile Association in 1913 and was the first physician in Toronto to make his rounds by automobile. He is also the man who bought the first used car in Canada, a one-cylinder Winton, from owner John Moodie of Hamilton. Doolittle was president of the CAA from 1920 to 1933.

Photo courtesy of the CAA Central Ontario.

DRIVING DOWN THE HIGHWAY

- If potholes get you down, consider this: the first recorded road in Canada was a sixteen-kilometre stretch of log surfaced road built by explorer Samuel de Champlain in 1606 between Port Royal and Digby Cape in what today is Nova Scotia.

- On May 1, 1900, in Winnipeg a horse buggy and a car collided in what was Canada's first recorded auto accident. No word on who got the worst of it.

- Canada's first concrete highway was built between Toronto and Hamilton in 1912 to accommodate a tremendous increase in traffic. In 1907, there were 2,130 cars on Canada's roads; five years later when the concrete highway was opened to traffic 50,000 cars were in use.

- In 1903, Ontario became the first province to issue car licences, which took the form of patent leather plaques with aluminum numbers. At the time, other provinces issued individual motorists a number for their vehicle and left it to the owners to make their own plates, usually from wood, metal, or leather.

- More than 17.5 million vehicles ply Canada's roads, including more than 16.5 million cars, vans, and small trucks weighing less than 4,500 kilograms; 320,000 medium-weight trucks weighing between 4,500 kilograms and 10,000 kilograms; 255,000 heavy trucks weighing in at more than 10,000 kilograms; and 74,000 buses.

- *Bad news and good news.* Although highway traffic in Canada has doubled over the past twenty-five years, there has been a 50 percent decline in traffic fatalities since the 1970s.

- About one hundred cars known as the London Six were made between 1921 and 1925 by London Motors Ltd. in London, Ontario. The cars featured an aluminum body over a wood frame supplied by a coffin maker.

> In 2003, Canadians who drove eighteen thousand kilometres during the course of the year paid an average of $19.32 per day to own their cars, based on the cost of insurance, licence, registration, depreciation, and a car loan, says the Canadian Automobile Association.

WHO WOULDA THUNK...

- The oldest drugstore in Canada is believed to be in Perth, Ontario. Originally opened by John Coombs in 1846, it has since been run by more than a dozen druggists. It now operates under the Pharmasave banner and has been completely modernized.

> Between 1949 and 1959, Canada's population rose from 13.5 million to 17.5 million, an increase of 29.6 percent. It was the largest increase in a single decade in Canadian history.

- *Facts about females.* Women typically outlive men by an average of six years. The average age of a widow in North America is fifty-eight. If a woman was

Dandelions, the yellow-flowered weed common in many Canadian lawns, first arrived in North America in the early 1600s aboard fishing vessels from Europe.

born between 1945 and 1965, she can expect to live into her 80s.

- A United church in the community of Actinolite in eastern Ontario is the only church in Canada constructed from marble. The Marble Church of Bridgewater, also known as the Actinolite United Church, was built in 1864, and thanks to its sturdy construction, survived a fire in 1889 that destroyed most of the village.

- The idea of operating food banks to help those in need was borrowed from the United States. It was first successfully developed in Canada in Edmonton.

- The Royal York Hotel once had its own private hospital with about a dozen beds in two wards.

Not your average hotel, the Royal York also once cared for the sick and infirm.

- Alzheimer's disease — a degenerative disease of the brain — could afflict more than 750,000 Canadians by 2031 as baby boomers age. Alzheimer's disease and related dementias already affect one in thirteen people older than sixty-five, and one in three of those eighty-five and older.

Branksome Hall, the famous Toronto girls' school, takes its name from the ancestral home of its first principal, Margaret Scott. It was another Scott, the writer Sir Walter Scott, who referred to the old castle home in a poem as "Branxholm Hall."

- The Yukon Territory had its own time zone until 1973, when it changed to Pacific Time.

- The idea of engineers wearing a ring on the baby finger of their dominant hand began in 1922 in Montreal. A group of engineers adopted the ring as a symbol of cohesiveness among their profession. Though known as the "iron ring," most rings are today made of stainless steel.

1. True or false? John Carling, who ran the Carling Brewery & Malting Company of London Ltd. in the late nineteenth century, never drank beer because it disagreed with his system.

2. In the 1990s, Interbrew S.A. became owner of the Toronto Blue Jays. In what country is this brewery based?

   a) Germany
   b) Luxembourg
   c) Ireland
   d) Belgium

3. Name the Waterloo, Ontario-based brewery that brought stubby beer bottles back to the market in spring 2002.

4. According to the Brewers Association of Canada, one of the main reasons American beer tastes different from the Canadian variety is that ours contains more malt barley. What do American brewers use more of?

   a) corn
   b) wheat
   c) rye
   d) oats

5. John Labatt Ltd. says its founder, John Kinder Labatt, is responsible for introducing the idea of a certain national holiday. Which one?

   a) Thanksgiving
   b) Victoria Day
   c) Labour Day
   d) Canada Day

   John Kinder Labatt gave us another holiday to celebrate.

Courtesy of Labatt Archives.

6. Before Eugene O'Keefe started the brewery that bears his name, he had a background in a different business. What was it?

   a) wine making
   b) farming
   c) banking
   d) horse breeding

QUIZ #11

A QUIZ FOR WHAT ALES YOU

Canadians love their beer, eh? Here's a case of twenty we hope you'll find refreshing. Cheers!

What was the slogan for Labatt 50?

7. Match the slogan to the brand of beer:

    a) 50   i) Hey Mabel, _____.
    b) Canadian   ii) _____ says it all.
    c) Budweiser   iii) Me and the boys and our ___.
    d) Black Label   iv) I am _____!
    e) Ex   v) _____, the King of Beers.

8. When George Sleeman ran the Sleeman Brewery in the late nineteenth century, it was said that the driveway leading up to his manor was inlaid with what?

    a) beer caps
    b) bottle openers
    c) beer barrels
    d) upturned beer bottles

9. In what city is Spinnakers IPA microbrewed?

    a) Halifax
    b) Victoria
    c) St. John's
    d) Charlottetown

10. What do the letters IPA stand for?

11. In the early 1980s, Canada's brewers abandoned stubby bottles in favor of "long neck" bottles because stubbies:

    a) broke easily
    b) fell out of fashion
    c) could not keep beer fresh for more than a week
    d) could not accommodate screw-off caps

12. Where was the first Canadian beer bottle produced?

    a) Toronto, Ontario
    b) Sherbrooke, Quebec
    c) Mallorytown, Ontario
    d) Halifax, Nova Scotia

13. In 1968, a regulation was passed in Manitoba that allowed patrons of beverage rooms to:

    a) drink beer without meals

b) stand up while drinking beer
c) drink beer on outdoor patios
d) purchase cases of beer on site for use at home

14. When John Molson began brewing beer in Montreal in 1786, what did a bottle of his ale cost?

a) five cents
b) seven cents
c) ten cents
d) twelve cents

15. Besides brewing, which of the following businesses has the Molson family been involved in over the years?

a) banking
b) chemicals
c) building supplies
d) railway
e) all of the above

16. What was the Labatt Streamliner?

a) a sleek beer bottle introduced in the 1970s by Labatt
b) a championship speedboat sponsored by the brewery
c) the name of Labatt's beer delivery trucks
d) the name of Labatt's corporate jet

17. Match the brewery with the province:

a) Creemore Springs Brewery Ltd.
b) Moosehead Brewing Company
c) Great Western Brewing Company Ltd.
d) Big Rock Brewery Ltd.

i)   Alberta
ii) Saskatchewan
iii) Ontario
iv) New Brunswick

18. What is mixed with beer to make a Twist Shandy?

a) tomato juice

b) lemon lime
c) orange juice
d) soda water

19. What was the name of Canada's first "light" beer?

a) Amstel Light
b) Carlsberg Light
c) Labatt's Cool Light
d) Oland's Lite

20. What was unique about Heidelberg beer?

a) the shape of the bottle
b) it was imported from Germany
c) it contained twice the alcohol content of most beers
d) it was the first Canadian beer with a label painted onto the bottle

 Answers can be found on page 124

FIRST OFF THE MARK

- Archie isn't just the name of a cartoon character; it's also the name of the world's first Internet search engine, developed in 1990 at McGill University in Montreal.

- A rail track laid in 1829 to haul coal at a Pictou, Nova Scotia, mine was the first track made from metal in Canada and possibly in North America. The tramway was operated using horses until 1838.

- Entrepreneur Henry Morgan opened Canada's first department store in Montreal in 1845 and called it, not surprisingly, Morgan's. By 1892, four others had followed — Eaton's, Simpson's, The Hudson's Bay Co., and Woodward's. Morgan's was bought by the Hudson's Bay Co. in 1960.

- The first train tunnel in British North America was built in Brockville, Ontario, between 1854 and 1860. The Brockville Railway Tunnel enabled Grand Trunk Railway trains to travel through a wedge of rock to the nearby waterfront. Victoria Hall, Brockville's city hall, was constructed on top of the tunnel in the early 1860s.

In 1884, the first Canadian wheat was shipped overseas. It was transported by rail from western Canada to Port Arthur (now Thunder Bay), then to Owen Sound by lake boat, and then to Montreal by rail, where it was loaded aboard an ocean steamship bound for Glasgow, Scotland.

Courtesy of the Brockville Museum.

The Brockville Railway Tunnel.

- *Planting the seed.* In 1861, George Lawson established the first botanical garden in Canada in Kingston, Ontario. The garden lasted only about a decade, but it predated the gardens set up at the Central Experimental Farm in Ottawa by about twenty-five years.

- Canada's first real estate board was set up in 1888 in Vancouver at a time when a commercial lot on Hornby Street near the Hotel Vancouver sold for $600. The Vancouver Board was active until the start of World War I, when operations were suspended. It resumed in 1919 and has been operating ever since.

Photo by Bryan Ray.

Vancouver was the site of Canada's first real estate board.

Once lucky, twice ... Matthew Webb, the first person to swim across the English Channel without a life jacket, tried to swim across the rapids and whirlpool below Niagara Falls in 1883. He drowned.

- In 1966, beer could be served with meals at Parliament Hill in Ottawa for the first time since the Centre Block burned down in 1916.

- Canada's oldest newspaper is the *Halifax Gazette*, first published on March 23, 1752. Since September 2002, a copy of the first edition of the paper has been part of the National Library's rare books collection in Ottawa. The one-sheet copy of the paper was purchased for $40,000 from the Massachusetts Historical Society.

- In 1892, the first Children's Aid Society shelter opened in Toronto after John Kelso, a police reporter for the *Toronto World*, was convinced the only way to help homeless children was to establish an organization that would care for them until they were adopted into stable families.

- Edmonton was the first city in North America with a population under 1 million to build a light rapid transit system, which opened to the public in April 1978.

- The first airmail flight in Canada took place in 1918. A military aircraft took off in Montreal in the morning with 120 letters, refuelled in Kingston, Ontario, and made its delivery in Toronto late that afternoon.

The first use of "Canada" as an official name came in 1791 when the Province of Quebec was divided into the colonies of Upper and Lower Canada. In 1841, the two Canadas were again united under one name, the Province of Canada. At the time of Confederation, the new country assumed the name of Canada.

- Canada's first wallpaper was made in 1842. During the following century, twelve manufacturing operations were launched, including several in Toronto and Montreal. At the end of the nineteenth century, papers costing five cents a roll were in greatest demand.

- The first Canadian city to have electric street lighting was Hamilton, Ontario, home of Canada's steel industry. Public electric lights were installed there in 1883, one year before Montreal and Toronto got them.

- Quebec City holds the distinction of building the first covered ice rink in the world in 1852. Natural ice was used in these early arenas; artificial ice rinks started in British Columbia in 1911–12.

- Bob Noorduyn was responsible for building the world's first bush plane in 1934. The plane met the need for a high-wing, single-engine aircraft that could carry heavy loads and get in and out of small places, particularly in Canada's north.

- Cecil Smith was the first woman to represent Canada in any Olympic event. She competed in figure skating at the 1924 Winter Olympics in Chamonix, France.

- John Cannon of Elora, Ontario, patented the world's first panoramic camera in 1888. It photographed 360 degrees in one exposure by advancing the film at the same speed the camera's lens moved.

> The first Canadian to be a Playboy Playmate was Pamela Anne Gordon, who bared all for the magazine back in March 1962. Several other Canadian women, notably Pamela Anderson, Dorothy Stratten, Shannon Tweed, and Kimberley Conrad have also posed nude for the magazine.

THOSE CRAZY CANUCKS AND THEIR CULTURE

- Francophone residents of Quebec are Canada's most avid viewers of television, watching an average of 26 hours each week, says Statistics Canada. The rest of Canada spends an average of 22.7 hours in front of the TV.

- Approximately 4.5 million Canadians are involved in hockey as coaches, players, officials, administrators, or direct volunteers. More than 540,000 players are registered with Hockey Canada, and between them they play more than 1.5 million games every season and take part in 2 million practices at Canada's 3,500 arenas.

- On average, Canadian households spend $257 a year on gaming, which includes the purchase of lottery tickets, casino gambling, and playing games of chance on video lottery terminals. Quebec leads the way, spending an average of $267 per family.

Casinos like this one attract millions of Canadians — and their wallets — each year.

SOME TANTALIZING TIDBITS

- Canadians love to drink their water, as evidenced by an 18 percent increase in the amount of bottled water consumed in 2003 over 2002. By comparison, milk drinkers downed 1 percent more milk over the same period, while the consumption of flavoured soft drinks fell by 2 percent.

Consumption of bottled water is growing at a much faster rate than that of the old standby, milk.

- In 1983, a huge Union Jack was wrapped around an entire house in St. John's, Newfoundland, to celebrate a visit by Queen Elizabeth during Newfoundland's four hundredth anniversary celebrations.

- After arriving by ship in Halifax and Quebec City, newcomers to Canada often headed west in wooden boxcars with a cookstove in the middle. Some disembarked at Montreal and Toronto to look for factory and mill jobs. Thousands more stayed on the trains in hope of finding jobs in fast-growing western towns or to try their hand at farming.

- Canada's oldest continuous town band, the Perth Citizens' Band, still performs regularly in the bandstand behind the town hall in Perth, Ontario.

> Police estimate there are more than ten thousand hydroponic marijuana laboratories hidden in homes across southern Ontario. With an average yield of more than twelve hundred plants a year, it's a $12-billion industry. Some say it's Ontario's largest cash crop.

DID YOU KNOW THAT ...

- *Bargoons.* In the early 1900s, a pair of shoes could be had for $2, a car cost $800, and cheese sold for $0.25. At the time, women earned, on average, $182.50 a year, and men earned $389. And ... there was no income tax.

- In 1900, Victoria Day was a big celebration of Canada's British heritage in many cities and towns. Three years earlier, Empire Day had been established to celebrate Queen Victoria's sixtieth year as the Queen of England. Empire Day was the school day before Victoria Day.

Queen Victoria mourned in 1901.

Courtesy of the National Archives of Canada, PA-028924.

> The last fatal duel in Canada was fought in Perth, Ontario, on June 13, 1833. It was fought between two young law students on the banks of the Tay River for a lady's honour. The victim of the duel, Robert Lyon, is buried in the Old Burying Ground, a Roman Catholic/Anglican/Presbyterian pioneer cemetery in Perth.

> Newcomers to Canada's Prairies, known as sod-busters, were sold a quarter section of land (160 acres or 65 hectares) for $10. Once on their land, the settlers would break the tough surface soil and cut it into bricks to build a shelter or "sod-die," which they called home for their first winter.

- Canadians spend nearly 90 percent of their time indoors, according to the Canada Mortgage and Housing Corporation, which says indoor air is sometimes two to five times more polluted than outside air, and, in extreme cases, as much as one hundred times dirtier.

- To save money, many companies in the early 1900s employed women and children where possible. In parts of Nova Scotia, 16 percent of the workforce consisted of children who fit into the small spaces in mines.

- More than 3 million Canadians are stricken with serious respiratory diseases such as asthma, lung cancer, influenza, pneumonia, tuberculosis, and cystic fibrosis. These and other respiratory ailments account for more than $12 billion in health care–related expenditures every year, including the cost of hospitalization, physician visits, and drugs.

QUIZ #12

THE RED AND WHITE FLAG FOREVER

Canada's maple leaf flag was raised at the Parliament Buildings in Ottawa for the first time on February 15, 1965, a bitterly cold winter day. We've been flying it proudly ever since. But how much do you know about this national icon that has been called "one of the world's great flags"?

We've run a few questions up the trivia flagpole to test your knowledge about the banner that is Canada's pre-eminent national symbol.

1. In what year did the federal government first begin searching for a new Canadian flag?

    a) 1963
    b) 1959
    c) 1925
    d) 1960

2. At Confederation in 1867, which flag was considered Canada's official flag, the Union Jack or the Red Ensign?

3. At game two of the 1992 World Series between Toronto and Atlanta and during Canada Day ceremonies on Parliament Hill on July 1, 1999, the Canadian flag was flown improperly. What was wrong?

    a) both flags were the wrong colour
    b) the flags were flown upside down
    c) improper flagpoles were used
    d) the flags were flown too low

4. Two members of the Group of Seven submitted designs to a Parliamentary Committee that was examining proposed designs for Canada's new flag. Which one of the following three artists did not suggest a design?

    a) A.Y. Jackson
    b) Lawren Harris
    c) A.J. Casson

5. Which national organization condemned Prime Minister Lester B. Pearson's promise in the mid-1960s to give Canadians a flag of their own?

    a) Canadian Automobile Association
    b) Royal Canadian Legion
    c) Canadian Medical Association
    c) Canadian Chamber of Commerce

6. How many red maple leaves were on Pearson's preferred design for a new Canadian flag, unveiled in May 1964?

    a) two
    b) one
    c) three
    d) five

7. What was the nickname given to Pearson's proposed flag design?

    a) Pearson's Pennant
    b) Red Cabbage

c)   the Maple Leaf Rag
d)   all of the above

8. Which of the following reasons were cited to con-
demn Pearson's plan to include the maple leaf on
Canada's new flag, according to *I Stand for Canada* by
Rick Archbold?

a)   The maple leaf did not represent the existence of
English and French Canada.
b)   The sugar maple tree didn't grow anywhere west
of the Ontario/Manitoba border.
c)   The Communist Party of Canada supported the flag.
d)   The sugar maple was the official tree of New York
State.
e)   All of the above.

9. Fill in the name on this declaration: I, _____,
Prime Minister of Canada, declare that February 15 will
be celebrated henceforth as National Flag of Canada
Day. Let us be proud of our flag!

10. What was the final alteration before the maple leaf flag
selected by a Parliamentary committee was adopted?

a)   the maple leaf was enlarged by one inch
b)   a deeper shade of red was used
c)   two points were removed from the base of the
maple leaf
d)   the stem of the maple leaf was shortened

**Canada's maple
leaf flag as it
appeared after
one final alter-
ation.**

Photo by Randy Ray.

11. What was the occupation of George Stanley in 1965 when he proposed the basic design that became Canada's red and white maple leaf flag?

    a) a senator in Manitoba
    b) a Halifax-based graphic artist
    c) a National Hockey League defenceman
    d) dean of the arts at Royal Military College in Kingston

12. What was flying atop the Peace Tower at Parliament Hill on February 15, 1965, before the first official raising of Canada's maple leaf flag took place?

    a) Union Jack
    b) nothing
    c) Red Ensign
    d) the governor general's standard

13. When former prime minister John Diefenbaker died, two flags were draped over his coffin as his body lay in state at Parliament Hill in August 1979. Which two?

    a) Canadian flag
    b) Saskatchewan provincial flag
    c) Red Ensign
    d) Union Jack

14. How does the federal government recommend Canadians dispose of a worn out Canadian flag?

    a) mail it to the Department of Canadian Heritage in Ottawa
    b) burn it
    c) shred it into tiny pieces
    d) take it to a landfill site

15. A version of the Union Jack is still found on the provincial flags of which four Canadian provinces?

    a) Ontario, Manitoba, Nova Scotia, and Saskatchewan
    b) Ontario, Manitoba, British Columbia, and Newfoundland
    c) Ontario, Alberta, Prince Edward Island, and Quebec
    d) Ontario, Alberta, Nova Scotia, and British Columbia

Ontario's flag.

16. The national flag is one of three of Canada's symbols of sovereignty. Pick the other two.

    a) the national coat of arms
    b) the Great Seal of Canada
    c) the House of Commons Mace
    d) the governor general's standard

 Answers can be found on page 125

QUIZ ANSWERS

QUIZ #11:
A QUIZ FOR WHAT ALES YOU

1. True.

2. d) Belgium.

3. Brick Brewing Co. Ltd., which reintroduced Red Cap Ale.

4. a) Corn.

5. b) Victoria Day.

6. c) Banking.

7. a) iii, b) iv, c) v, d) i, e) ii.

8. d) Upturned beer bottles.

9. b) Victoria.

10. India Pale Ale.

11. b) It fell out of fashion because brewers wanted more distinctive packaging.

12. c) Mallorytown, Ontario, at Mallorytown Glass Works, where bottles were blown by hand.

13. b) Stand up while drinking beer and carrying a glass around the room.

14. a) Five cents.

15. e) All of the above.

16. c) Labatt's beer delivery truck, first unveiled in 1936.

17. a) Alberta iii) Big Rock Brewery Ltd.
    b) Saskatchewan iv) Great Western Brewing Company Ltd.
    c) Ontario ii) Creemore Springs Brewery Ltd.
    d) New Brunswick i) Moosehead Breweries Limited.

18. b) Lemon lime.

19. c) Cool Light, which was test marketed by Labatt's in 1972 in British Columbia and Alberta.

20. a) It was sold in keg-shaped bottles from 1970 until 1972.

QUIZ #12:
THE RED AND WHITE FLAG FOREVER

1. c) 1925, when a committee of the Privy Council began to research possible designs for a national flag but never completed its work.

2. The Union Jack.

3.   b) The flags were flown upside down.

4.   b) Lawren Harris.

5.   b) Royal Canadian Legion.

6.   c) Three.

7.   d) All of the above.

8.   e) All of the above.

Jean Chrétien.

9. Jean Chrétien, on Feb. 15, 1996.

Photo by J.M. Carisse, courtesy of the Office of the Prime Minister.

10.   c) Two points were removed from the base of the maple leaf, reducing the number of points to eleven from thirteen.

11.   d) He was dean of the arts at Royal Military College.

12.   d) The governor general's standard.

Where did this flag last fly?

Courtesy of the Office of the Secretary to the Governor General.

13. a) The Canadian flag, and c) the Red Ensign.

14. b) A flag no longer suitable for use should be destroyed "in a dignified way by burning it privately," according to the Department of Canadian Heritage.

15. b) Ontario, Manitoba, British Columbia, and Newfoundland, which has a stylized version of the Union Jack.

Courtesy of Newfoundland and Labrador Tourism.

The Newfoundland flag.

16. a) The national coat of arms, and b) the Great Seal of Canada.

CHAPTER SIX

THIS LAND IS OUR LAND

For decades, the word "Canada" has conjured up visions of frozen tundra, abundant forests and minerals, sparkling lakes, endless prairies, and snowcapped mountains. But the land that makes up this vast country is renowned for more than fine game hunting and fishing, mineral-laden mines, and towering trees.

Did you know Canada lays claims to the world's largest lift lock and has the world's largest freshwater sand bar and dune system? Or that Canada has more than nine hundred thousand kilometres of roads and highways and a national highway system that is more than twenty-four thousand kilometres in length? And where else but in Canada would you find an island called "Donut"?

Read on to discover some of the great variety of landscapes, climates, transportation routes, and meteorological events that are integral parts of this sprawling country.

ROCKS AND ROLLS

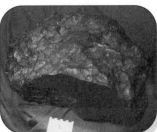

The largest meteorite found in Canada.

Photo by Dr. Richard Herd, Geological Survey of Canada/ NRCan.

- The largest meteorite discovered in Canada, an iron variety, was found near the town of Madoc, Ontario, in 1854. Known as the Madoc meteorite, it weighed 167.8 kilograms and is believed to have fallen to earth about fifty years earlier. It was acquired by the Geological Survey of Canada in 1855 and is on permanent exhibit in Logan Hall, National Resources Canada, in Ottawa.

- In 1956, the Thompson nickel deposit was discovered in Manitoba. Known as the Thompson Nickel Belt, it has yielded nickel from six mines and is Canada's second most important nickel mining area.

- *Shakin' all over.* The most powerful earthquake to shake Canada in the twentieth century was in 1949 off the Queen Charlotte Islands in British Columbia. It measured 8.1 on the Richter scale and was so severe that cows grazing on the islands were knocked off their feet and people could not stand. Damage was not high because of the area's sparse population at the time.

- With sales of about $1 billion, Canada in 2003 over-took South Africa to become the third-largest produc-er of diamonds in the world by value, after Botswana and Russia. In early 2004, Canada's two operating diamond mines were in the Northwest Territories, where two more are expected to open by 2006. Exploration and development of new mines is also underway in Nunavut and Northern Ontario.

- *Shine on.* The diamond was adopted as the official gemstone of the Northwest Territories on September 9, 1999, to recognize the NWT as home to Canada's first diamond mine.

> Lac de Pingualuit, a crater lake in northern Quebec's Ungava Peninsula, was formed when a meteorite smashed into the landscape a million years ago, leaving a depression twenty city blocks wide and deep enough to swallow the Empire State Building. The force of the explosion was thousands of times greater than that of the bomb that fell on Hiroshima.

GRAIN ELEVATORS, BEAVERS, AND ... PINGOS?

- Canada's first grain elevator, a round structure, was built in Nigerville, Manitoba, in 1879. It was the Ogilvie flour company that built the first of the rec-tangular, pitch-roofed grain elevators that became a common sight in communities across the Prairies. That elevator was built in Gretna, Manitoba, in 1881.

Courtesy of Agriculture and Agri-Food Canada.

Courtesy of Agriculture and Agri-Food Canada.

Grain elevators are becoming a thing of the past.

> In 1910, when beavers were beginning to over-run Ontario's Algonquin Park, live trapping of these and other species became a lucrative project to meet the demand for zoo animals from all over North America.

- The first bird sanctuary in North America was established in 1887 at Last Mountain Lake in Saskatchewan. It now forms the Last Mountain Lake National Wildlife Area.

- The Peterborough Lift Lock on the Trent-Severn Waterway at Peterborough, Ontario, is the highest hydraulic lift in the world. Work began in 1896, and when the job was completed in 1904 it enabled boaters to overcome a difference in elevation of more than nineteen metres between Little Lake and Nassau Mills.

- Before the cardinal was named after its red-robed counterparts in the Roman Catholic church, this popular backyard bird was called simply the "red-bird" by early settlers to North America.

- *Now, that's a freezer.* Pingos are ice-cored hills unique to permafrost areas in Canada's north. They form when underground ice expands and pushes upward on the ground to form a mound as high as fifty metres and up to three hundred metres in diameter. With some fourteen hundred pingos, the Tuktoyaktuk Peninsula in the Northwest Territories has the world's largest concentration of the hills. Before the arrival of freezers the Inuit used them to preserve food.

Pingos: ice-cored hills in Canada's north.

Courtesy of RWED, GNWT.

- One of Exeter, Ontario's claims to fame is that it's home to a rare type of white squirrel. Though they are a genetic anomaly, these squirrels are not albinos.

- The arbutus, Canada's only evergreen hardwood, is found only on the west coast. Its distinctive features are red bark and glossy green, oval-shaped leaves.

> Canada has three known major salt formations. In Western Canada, salt beds extend from the Northwest Territories, through Alberta, Saskatchewan, and into Manitoba, covering an area of approximately 390,000 square kilometres. In Ontario, salt is found in a deposit known as the Michigan Basin, underlying parts of Michigan, Ohio, and lakes Huron and Erie. In the Atlantic provinces it's found under New Brunswick, Nova Scotia, part of Newfoundland, and the Gulf of Saint Lawrence.

WAY UP NORTH

- The largest ice caps in the High Arctic are found on Ellesmere Island, where they can be more than a kilometre thick and cover some twenty thousand square kilometres, more than three times the area of Prince Edward Island.

- The Dempster Highway is the only Canadian highway that crosses the Arctic Circle. It runs for 741 kilometres, from just east of Dawson to Inuvik, but the most northerly leg is accessible only in winter when the Mackenzie River is frozen. Because it's a gravel road with few services, travellers need to carry spare tires, extra fuel, and other supplies.

The Ekati diamond mine northeast of Yellowknife, Northwest Territories, is the largest construction project north of the Canadian tree line. It opened in 1998 at a cost of $1 billion.

Spare tires needed on this highway.

With an area of 507,451 square kilometres (184,000 square miles) Baffin Island in Canada's north is big enough to hold Ireland, the United Kingdom, Hungary, and Austria combined and still have room left over. Yet the island has only twenty-eight settlements, including Iqaluit, the capital of Nunavut.

Alert, a small village in Nunavut, is the most northerly permanent settlement in the world. It was set up as a weather station in 1950 and was taken over by the military in 1958.

- *The bear facts.* The constellations Ursa Major and Ursa Minor (Latin for "great bear" and "little bear") permanently dominate the firmament of Canada's Far North. Because of their constant presence, the region that lies within the boreal polar circle is called the "Arctic," from "arktos," the Greek word for "bear."

- Permafrost, which is ground that remains at or below 0° C continuously for at least two years, underlies 40 to 45 percent of Canada and is beneath about 25 percent of the earth's surface. It may be composed of cold, dry earth; cold, wet earth; ice-cemented rock; or frozen subsurface and surface water.

- The Arctic ecozones, which have the lowest precipitation in Canada, encompass the Arctic islands as well as the northern portion of the continent from the Yukon Territory to Labrador. Average annual temperatures range between -17° C and -7° C, depending on the region, causing permafrost to be as much as several hundred metres deep.

- *Gold fever.* During the peak of the Klondike gold rush in 1903, $12 million worth of gold was discovered. By 1914, that figure had dropped to $5 million and continued to go downhill after that.

POINTS TO PONDER

- At 550 metres above sea level, the Ottawa Valley town of Foymount is the highest in Ontario. In the 1950s, during the Cold War, it was a radar station; today its height makes it a stargazing mecca for amateur astronomers.

- Canada's overall population density is about three people per square kilometre, but more than 85 percent of Canadians live within a three-hundred-kilo-metre strip along the Canada–United States border. In this area, the density is twenty-five persons per square kilometre, about the same as in the U.S.

- After Russia, Canada has the largest continuous forested area on earth. Covering nearly half the nation's land mass and constituting 10 percent of the globe's forest cover, Canada's forests shelter two hundred thousand plant and animal species and provide one of every seventeen Canadian jobs.

Forests continue to be an important part of Canada's economy.

- *Caught mapping.* The Canadian Atlas, the world's first complete national atlas, was put together in 1905 in Ottawa by federal government geographers and cartographers.

- The boundaries of Algonquin Park in Ontario were fixed in 1893 as an area of eighteen rectangular townships containing the headwaters of seven rivers.

- Craters on the moon are generally named for deceased scientists. Among the Canadians so honoured are Sir Frederick Banting, the co-discover of insulin; F.S. Hogg, who received the first doctorate in astronomy awarded by Harvard; astrophysicist Andrew McKellar; and astronomer J.S. Plaskett.

- The Douglas fir takes its name from David Douglas, a Scotsman who came to Canada in the early 1800s

When it comes to place names it's important to keep your Georges straight. Georgian Bay was named after King George IV, while the Strait of Georgia in British Columbia is named for George III.

and introduced some 250 plants to Europe from North America, more than any other person.

- The origin of the name "Calgary" seems to be in dispute. While scholars agree that it's a Gaelic word, some say it means "bay farm," others argue that it means "clear running water," while still others contend that it's defined as "the haven by the wall."

- Due to erosion, the falls at Niagara are about eleven kilometres from their place of origin at the present-day community of Queenston. The falls erode the soft shale and limestone they spill over by 1.2 metres every year.

The Falls lose ground every year.

Photo by Randy Ray.

- *Just how big are we?* Canada has a land mass of 9,970,610 square kilometres, making it the second-largest country in the world, after Russia. From east to west, Canada encompasses six time zones. Should Quebec ever separate, we'd drop to number five because China, the United States, and Brazil would leap over us.

- Newfoundland isn't the only place in the world with a half-hour time zone. Suriname in South America lies in the same zone. Parts of Asia and the Pacific Islands also have this curious time difference.

- Though it's called the Canadian River, it's found in the southwestern U.S. The river flows from south Colorado across New Mexico and northwest Texas to Oklahoma.

1. True or false? There are fewer than twenty species of ferns found in Canada.

2. Before it was renamed Lake Louise in 1882, what was this beautiful body of water in Alberta called?

   a) Shining Lake
   b) Lake Wilson
   c) Banff Lake
   d) Emerald Lake

3. Which of the following bridges does not connect the Niagara Falls, Ontario, area to the United States?

   a) Ivy Lea
   b) Rainbow
   c) Whirlpool
   d) Queenston-Lewiston

4. "Rock doctor" is a Canadian slang term for which profession?

   a) disk jockey
   b) geologist
   c) jeweller
   d) highway construction worker

5. Unscramble the following words to come up with animals found in Canada.

   a) obraciu
   b) darbeg
   c) toyeco
   d) lewayle

6. I'm a period of six or more hours with winds above forty kilometres per hour, visibility reduced below one kilometre by blowing or drifting snow, and temperatures below -12° C. What am I?

 Answers can be found on page 159

QUIZ #13

SIX TO SAVOUR

With a country that stretches from sea to sea, there shouldn't be any trouble unearthing a few trivial treasures. See how you do with these.

MORE NUGGETS OF NATURE

a Prince Edward Island began as three islands. When glaciers of the last ice age melted, the water level in the Atlantic Ocean rose and only one island remained, likely about three thousand years ago.

> According to Native legend, the thirty thousand islands in Ontario's Georgian Bay were created when Kitchi-Kiwana, the last of a race of giants, fell with a mountain in his arms, which shattered into thirty thousand pieces.

• The first printed maps to show the New World appeared around 1506. They depicted Newfoundland being joined to Greenland, which was shown as an extension of Asia. The concept of Greenland and Newfoundland being separate from Asia became popular with mapmakers about a decade later.

• Native peoples discovered the Great Lakes, but the man generally credited with the European "discovery" of the lakes is Étienne Brûlé, a French scout for Samuel de Champlain. Brûlé reached Georgian Bay on Lake Huron around 1615.

• *Seaside stamp store.* The only post office in a lighthouse in North America is found in Peggy's Cove, Nova Scotia. The lighthouse no longer serves its original purpose of guiding boats and is only used as a post office in the summer during peak tourist times.

Photo by Harold Wright.

Canada's postal lighthouse.

• Queen Victoria Park in Niagara Falls, Ontario, was created in 1887, becoming Canada's first provincial park. It was designed to save the area from hucksters and promoters.

• The honour of Canada's southernmost town goes to Kingsville, Ontario. Located in Essex County east of Windsor, Kingsville is a centre for bird-watching, fishing, agriculture, and automotive-related industries.

- *Fruit of the loam.* The fertile lands of the Okanagan Valley in British Columbia produce 100 percent of Canada's apricots and about one-third each of this country's apples, pears, plums, peaches, and sweet and sour cherries.

- Toronto Island is actually an archipelago of fifteen islands in Lake Ontario. The eight largest islands are Centre, Muggs, Donut (the one with the hole in the middle), Forestry, Olympic, South, Snake, and Algonquin.

- On average, forest fires in Canada destroy twice the number of trees harvested by the country's forest industry.

- Canada's first national park is Banff National Park, which was established in 1885, originally to protect the hot springs near Sulphur Mountain.

- Saskatchewan has more than one-third of all the farmland in Canada, with more than a quarter million square kilometres. With only 335 square kilometres, Newfoundland, also known as The Rock, has the least amount of farmland of any province, including Prince Edward Island. In PEI, about 5,660 square kilometres of land are used for farming.

How times have changed. Though it wasn't an official event, the forerunner of the International Plowing Match in Ontario took place in 1846 on a farm near the intersection of what today is Yonge Street and St. Clair Avenue in Toronto. The first official International Plowing Match was held in 1913 on the site where Toronto's Sunnybrook Hospital is located.

Despite the country's increasing population, approximately 89 percent of Canada has never been permanently settled.

Courtesy of Newfoundland and Labrador Tourism.

Farmland is scarce in Newfoundland.

- *The long and winding roads.* Canada has more than nine hundred thousand kilometres of roads and highways and a national highway system that is more than twenty-four thousand kilometres in length.

Hundreds of highways criss-cross Canada for thousands of kilometres.

Canada occupies half of North America and nearly 7 percent of the total surface of the earth.

- Though ginseng is a popular crop in British Columbia, it was common to Ontario in the early 1700s and was found in the woods of central and eastern North America. In China, which is a large market for British Columbia ginseng, the crop is often referred to as the "elixir of life" because of its many purported medicinal benefits.

Life's a beach. Sandbanks Provincial Park on Lake Ontario has the world's largest freshwater sand bar and dune system.

- Although the Canadian Horseshoe Falls at Niagara Falls are considered by most to be more spectacular, the falls on the American side, at sixty-four metres high, are about ten metres higher than those on the Canadian side.

- Though it is plagued by pollution and lampreys, Lake Erie supports the largest commercial fishery of all the

Despite its troubled history, Lake Erie continues to be a popular source for commercial fishing.

Great Lakes. More than twenty thousand tonnes of fish, mostly yellow perch, are caught there annually.

- The terrain stretching from northern Africa to Scandinavia bears a striking resemblance to the Atlantic shores of the Maritimes and Newfoundland because they were once part of the same land mass. The continents split apart 200 million years ago.

> In Canada, correctly placed deciduous trees can shade a home in a way that reduces air conditioning needs by up to 75 percent. And a fifty-foot-by-fifty-foot patch of lawn releases enough oxygen daily to meet the needs of a family of four.

THE NAME'S FAMILIAR: HOW THE PROVINCES AND TERRITORIES WERE NAMED

- Newfoundland: Because John Cabot was considered to have found this "new isle," it was first called "Terra Nova" before the English "Newfoundland" became more popular.

Once known as Terra Nova.

Courtesy of Newfoundland and Labrador Tourism.

- Prince Edward Island: Its original British name was the Island of Saint John, but in 1799 it was changed to its present name to honour a son of King George III, who was stationed with the British army in Halifax at the time.

The wide, sandy beaches of Prince Edward Island attract tourists from around the world.

- Nova Scotia: From the Latin for "New Scotland," it was officially named when King James I, a Scot, was on the throne of England.

Canada's New Scotland.

Courtesy of Nova Scotia Tourism and Culture.

- New Brunswick: It was named in 1784 after the German duchy of Brunswick-Lunenburg, which was also ruled at that time by King George III of England.

- Quebec: First applied to the city only and then later to the province, it comes from an Algonquian word meaning "where the river narrows."

The Chateau Frontenac Hotel in Quebec City is one of the province's most familiar landmarks.

- Ontario: Possibly derived from the Iroquois word "kanadario," meaning sparkling or beautiful water. May also mean "beautiful lake" or "large body of water," given that the name was given to the Great Lake first and later to the land near it.

- Manitoba: A word that means "where the spirit lives" in the languages of the province's Aboriginal people.

- Saskatchewan: Derived from the Plains Indian word "kisiskatchewan," which means "swiftly flowing river." Saskatchewan is also the name of the major river system in the province.

- Alberta: Named after Princess Louise Caroline Alberta, fourth daughter of Queen Victoria.

- British Columbia: Stems from the province's intense "Britishness" in its early years and originated with Queen Victoria. The name was officially proclaimed in 1858.

- Yukon: From the Loucheux Native name Yu-kun-tah for the "great river" (Yukon River) that drains most of its area.

- Northwest Territories: Describes the territory acquired in 1870 from the Hudson's Bay Company and Great Britain, Rupert's Land and the North-Western Territory, which was located northwest of Central Canada.

> Nunavut: Means "our land" in Inuktitut, the Inuit language. It officially became a territory on April 1, 1999.

CANUCK CRITTERS

- The beaver attained official status as an emblem of Canada when an "act to provide for the recognition of the beaver (*castor canadensis*) as a symbol of the sovereignty of Canada" received royal assent on March 24, 1975.

- *Lotsa legs.* There are about seventy species of centipedes found in Canada, the largest being about eight centimetres long. The house centipede is the only species in Canada that has a bite painful to humans.

There are no rats in Alberta thanks to a program created in the mid-1950s by the Alberta Department of Agriculture. The program, using traps and poison, was concentrated along the Saskatchewan border to keep rats from entering the province.

- Cnidarians are the only jellyfish found in Canada's freshwater lakes and rivers, though it's not clear whether they are native to this country. They're shaped like a parachute, able to grow as big as a quarter, and are found in only twenty lakes, mostly in southern Quebec, where the water is less acidic.

- Atlantic salmon are found in about three hundred rivers in Labrador, Quebec, and the Maritimes. They were also commonly found in Lake Ontario until the late nineteenth century.

- There are approximately one thousand species of bees in Canada; some can even be found north of the Arctic Circle. Among the species that live here are bumblebees, honeybees, cuckoo, sweat, and mining bees.

- *What's good for the goose.* In 1950, there were 1 million Canada geese in North America. Today, the Canadian Wildlife service estimates there are 5 million, crediting the increased numbers to restrictions on hunting and the establishment of new colonies.

Canada geese thrive in the country that gave them their name.

Photo by Mark Kearney.

- Atlantic sturgeon, the largest fish in the St. Lawrence River, have been known to live for up to sixty years, reach 4.5 metres in length, and weigh up to 360 kilograms.

ONLY IN CANADA, YOU SAY? FIVE FOUR-LEGGED FRIENDS UNIQUE TO THIS COUNTRY

- The Tahltan Bear Dog: This small dog with white and black patches and a distinctive tail that ends in a wide brush is extinct in this country. It was kept by the Tahltan Indians of northwestern British Columbia for use mainly as hunters of bear and lynx and was once recorded by the *Guinness Book of Records* as the world's rarest breed.

© Canada Post Corporation, 1988. Reproduced with permission.

37 Canada

Tahltan Bear Dog • Chien d'ours de Tahltan

Canada's bear dog.

- Nova Scotia Duck Tolling Retriever: Foxlike in colour and intermediate in size, the tolling retriever's roots trace back to Yarmouth County, Nova Scotia, where the breed was developed in the late nineteenth century. Several breeds and crosses were key to its evolution, including the Irish setter, which gave the breed its colour, and the yellow farm collie, the source of its bushy tail. Among the Toller's most unique attributes is its ability to mimic the behaviour of a fox to draw waterfowl within the firing range of hunters.

Photo by Randy Ray.

The Duck Tolling Retriever.

- Canadian Eskimo Dog: Used mainly as a sled and backpack dog, this is the only breed of dog associated with the Aboriginal peoples of the Arctic. The history of this powerfully built canine dates back between eleven hundred and two thousand years, when it was taken to the North American Arctic by the Thule Eskimos and gradually spread to Greenland. The Canadian Eskimo Dog is intermediate in speed and strength and in all seasons is a hunting companion with a nose keen enough to locate seal breathing holes in the ice and brave enough to hold large game at bay until the hunter comes in for the kill.

Newfoundland: According to Newfoundland folklore, the breed's progenitor was the Tibetan Mastiff, which had migrated across the Canadian north to Newfoundland and into Viking settlements before being crossed with the Viking bear dog in AD 1001. Known as the "gentle giant" of Canadian breeds, the heavy, long-coated dogs are excellent swimmers and are renowned as family companions and guardians with strong life-saving instincts.

- Labrador Retriever: The Labrador, whose ancestors were discovered in Newfoundland and Labrador by eighteenth-century colonists, is thought to have descended from dogs abandoned in the region by European fishermen. In the early 1800s, specimens were taken to Britain where they were crossed with other retrievers to become the most valued game dog in the country. Skilful hunters known for their intelligence and gentle, affectionate natures, the Labrador is one of the best gundogs in existence and is used extensively as a "seeing eye" dog. Most are black but some are yellow, chocolate, and cream.

MORE CANADIAN CREATURES

- *Cross-border birds.* Though cardinals are a common sight in Canadian backyards, the colourful birds are not native to this country. They moved here from the U.S. in the early 1900s.

- Approximately 140 species of grasshopper are found in Canada, and they range through every province in this country. About twelve thousand species are found around the world.

- The Chapleau Game Preserve and Wildlife Sanctuary in Northern Ontario, which is about 800,000 hectares (about 1.9 million acres), is the largest game preserve in the world. Creatures seen there include wolves, various birds of prey, otters, mink, fox, moose, and black bears.

- *Don't ever forget.* Jumbo, the famous circus elephant of the nineteenth century, was killed in St. Thomas, Ontario, after colliding with a locomotive. Jumbo was being led along the tracks on September 15, 1885, when an unscheduled train appeared out of the fog and collided with him. One hundred years after his death, a life-size statue of the elephant was erected in St. Thomas.

A real stud. Starbuck, a Canadian bull who sired two hundred thousand dairy cows and an equal number of bulls in his life, earned an estimated $25 million before he died in 1998. After his death, his frozen semen continued to sell for $250 a dose.

Jumbo's statue greets visitors in St. Thomas, Ontario, where the famous elephant was killed.

- Since the 1980s, a wide array of unusual creatures has been found on Canadian farms, including elks, emus, ostriches, wild boars, and llamas. In fact, farmers across Canada are tending more than one hundred species of exotic creatures, mainly because of changes in consumer preferences.

- Slippery, a famous sea lion from London, Ontario, made international headlines in 1958 by escaping from the city's Storybook Gardens and swimming down the Thames River. He was later captured in Lake Erie near Sandusky, Ohio, and brought home. His exploits were later turned into a documentary and stage play.

Visitors to Storybook Gardens pass by this statue of Slippery the sea lion near the front entrance.

- The peregrine falcon, which makes its home in Canada's Yukon Territory, is among the fastest creatures on earth, capable of flying two hundred kilometres per hour.

- Nova Scotia was the first province to choose an official bird. It is the osprey, a fish-eating species with long, sharp talons. There are some 250 active osprey nests in the province.

The waters of the Pacific Ocean off the coast of British Columbia are home to the world's largest species of octopus, *octopus dofleini*. This eight-armed creature can grow up to nine metres wide and weigh more than one hundred kilograms.

- Canada's beef cattle population amounts to 13 million head, and dairy cows number 1.3 million. The Canadian swine inventory exceeds 12 million head.

- The bison, or North American buffalo, is the largest native land animal in Canada. A mature male can be 3.8 metres long, 1.8 metres tall at the shoulder, and weigh up to 720 kilograms.

- About 650 million animals are killed for food in Canada each year. In many cases, the animals are kept in cages or stalls their entire lives to provide such foods as eggs and meat.

1. True or false? The ten highest mountains in Canada are all located in the Yukon.

2. Who owns the North Pole?

   a) Canada
   b) the United States
   c) the United Nations
   d) no one

3. Name the only two Canadian provinces that do not have a coast on salt water.

4. Why is the historic Chateau Montebello hotel on the Ottawa River between Montreal and Ottawa referred to as "a seventh wonder of the world"?

Courtesy of Fairmont Le Château Montebello.

The Chateau Montebello hotel.

   a) It was built using ten thousand logs from British Columbia.
   b) It is built on a swamp.
   c) It is the largest hotel in the world.
   d) It was built in two months.

5. Which is longer, the St. Lawrence River or the MacKenzie River?

 Answers can be found on page 159

QUIZ #14

**COAST-
TO-
COAST
QUIZ**

You're an expert in Canadian geography, eh? Then try these questions on for size!

BACK TO THE LAND

- About 7 percent of Canada's land mass, or 68 million hectares, is farmed. That's an area of land equal to nearly all of Germany and Japan combined. The Prairie provinces of Alberta, Saskatchewan, and Manitoba contain 80 percent of the land in Canada that is used for farming.

Dr. Charles Saunders helped open Canada's west.

Courtesy of Agriculture and Agri-Food Canada.

- Marquis wheat gets credit for bringing prosperity to Canada's prairies in the early 1900s. Its creator was Dr. Charles Saunders of London, Ontario, whose superior strain of wheat matured earlier than other varieties and resisted harsh weather.

- The Carolinian Zone, which stretches through southwestern Ontario near Lake Erie, contains more types of flora and fauna than anywhere else in the country. Among the warm-weather species found there are cucumber trees, wild turkeys, sassafras, opossums, and the red mulberry, considered to be the rarest tree in Canada.

The strongest currents in the world are the Nakwakto Rapids at Slingsby Channel in British Columbia. The flow rate can reach sixteen knots, or more than eighteen miles per hour. Canada is also home to the world's largest tides at the Bay of Fundy. The range from low to high tide is greater than sixteen metres.

- Kicking Horse Pass, which cuts through the Rocky Mountains near Lake Louise, Alberta, was named by naturalist Dr. James Hector. It seems Hector was kicked in the chest by one of his packhorses while exploring the area in August 1858.

- At fourteen hundred kilometres long, the Rocky Mountain Trench is the longest valley in North America. It runs northwest to southeast, almost completely through British Columbia from Montana to the Liard Plain just south of the B.C.-Yukon border.

- *Look way up.* The tallest tree in Canada is a Sitka spruce in British Columbia's Carmanah Pacific Provincial Park. It towers nearly ninety-six metres above the ground.

- Prince Edward Island, with its rich red soil, is Canada's smallest province, making up a mere 0.1 percent of Canada's land mass.

- The Grand Banks have been called the "wheat fields" of Newfoundland. The shallow continental shelf extends four hundred kilometres off the east coast, where the mixing of ocean currents has created one of the richest fishing grounds in the world. Once thought to contain a virtually inexhaustible supply of fish, the banks are now a vulnerable resource that must be wisely managed.

From sea to sea … to sea? Canada's motto, "From sea to sea," is geographically inaccurate. In addition to its coastlines on the Atlantic and Pacific, Canada has a third sea coast on the Arctic Ocean, giving it the longest coastline of any country.

Courtesy of Newfoundland and Labrador Tourism.

Fishing is in trouble on the Grand Banks.

Courtesy of Newfoundland and Labrador Tourism.

- Canada boasts the longest highway in the world, the Trans-Canada Highway, which runs 7,821 kilometres between Victoria, B.C., and St. John's, Newfoundland, as well as one of the busiest sections of highway in the world, Highway 401 through the Greater Toronto Area. On a typical day, more than four hundred thousand vehicles use Highway 401 where it intersects with Highway 400.

WATER, WATER, EVERYWHERE

The Canadian falls at Niagara are spectacular, but they are far from the highest in Canada. There are twelve other waterfalls in the country with higher vertical drops, led by Della Falls at Della Lake, B.C., at 440 metres and Takakkaw Falls at Daly Glacier, also in B.C., at 244 metres. Canada's Horseshoe Falls in Niagara sends water plummeting fifty-seven metres.

- There are about 2 million lakes in Canada, covering about 7.6 percent of the country's land mass. The main lakes, in order of the amount of surface area located in Canada, are Huron, Great Bear, Superior, Great Slave, Winnipeg, Erie, and Ontario. The largest lake situated entirely in Canada is Great Bear Lake, 31,326 square kilometres, located in the Northwest Territories.

- The largest lake within a lake in Canada is Lake Manitou, covering 106.42 square kilometres and found on Manitoulin Island in Lake Huron.

- *Us versus U.S.* When it comes to water volume, Canada's side of Niagara Falls is the clear winner. The Horseshoe Falls has a flow of 155 million litres per minute, compared to 14 million litres per minute on the American side.

- *And the bronze medal goes to …* Most people know that the Mackenzie and St. Lawrence rivers are the two longest in Canada, but did you know that the third longest is the Nelson River, which is 2,575 kilometres long and flows into Hudson Bay? The Yukon River is actually longer, but only 1,149 kilometres are within Canada.

Lake Superior is big enough to contain the other four Great Lakes plus three additional lakes the size of Lake Erie.

- Lake Superior is the deepest of the Great Lakes, with a maximum depth of 406 metres. The shallowest of the five lakes is Lake Erie, which is 64 metres deep. Lake Huron is 229 metres deep, Lake Ontario is 243 metres deep, and Lake Michigan is 282 metres deep.

- Hydrologically speaking, lakes Michigan and Huron are actually one lake, separated by the Straits of Mackinaw. The Mackinac Bridge, nicknamed the

"Mighty Mac," spans the straits, connecting Michigan's upper and lower peninsulas.

- The Great Lakes are the largest bodies of fresh water in the world. They are said to hold enough water to cover all the land in Canada to a depth of three metres and drain an area larger than Great Britain and France combined.

> Though you wouldn't know it to look at it today, in the late 1700s, Toronto's Don River had an excellent salmon fishery, which made the river a selling feature for properties in the area.

NAME THAT LAKE

Since the early 1600s, the Great Lakes have been tagged with numerous monikers, depending on who was drafting maps or writing about them. Pick your favourite!

- In 1632, French explorer Samuel de Champlain called Lake Ontario "Lake St. Louis"; Lake Huron, "Mer Douce"; and Lake Michigan, the "Grand Lac."

- A map drawn by French geographer Nicholas Sanson in 1656 calls Ontario "Lac de St. Louis"; Erie, "Lac du Chat"; Huron, "Karegnondi"; Michigan, "Lac de Puans"; and Superior, "Lac Supérieur."

- A map made in 1660 by Crexius calls the Great Lakes Lacus Ontarius, Lacus Erius seu Felis, Mare Dulce seu Lacus Huronum, Magnus Lacus Algonquinorum seu Lacus Foetetium, and Lacus Superior.

> Lake Michigan was once named "Lake of the Stinking Water" or "Lake of the Puans," after the Winnebago Indians who occupied its shores and were known to some as the "Ouinpegouek," or "people of the stinking water," a name that referred to the smelly algae-rich waters nearby. In the mid-1600s, it was also designated as Lac St. Joseph and Lac Dauphin. Through the further explorations of Jolliet and Marquette, it received its final name, Lake Michigan.

- On a Jesuit map from 1672, Lake Michigan is "Lac des Illinois" and Lake Superior is "Lake Tracy." The first French explorers referred to Superior as le lac superieur, which translates to "Upper Lake," that is, the lake above Lake Huron. The Chippewa called Superior "Kitchi-gummi" (or "Kitchi-gami"), signifying great water or great lake.

WACKY WEATHER

- Canada's most disastrous tornado struck Regina, Saskatchewan, on June 30, 1912, when the Regina "Cyclone" left at least twenty-eight dead and hundreds injured.

- On October 15, 1954, Hurricane Hazel swept across Toronto, dumping 178 millimetres of rain, killing 83 people, and destroying entire streets in the west part of the city. Hazel remains Canada's worst inland storm.

Debris is cleared in the wake of Hurricane Hazel.

Courtesy of the National Archives of Canada, PA-174539.

- Though Hurricane Hazel is the best-known storm to hit Canada, others have been deadlier. A cyclone in August 1873 in the Maritimes destroyed twelve hundred ships, while another that struck Newfoundland in September 1775 led to the drowning of several thousand British sailors.

- Landslides and snow avalanches have resulted in more than six hundred deaths in Canada since 1850 and have caused billions of dollars of direct and indirect damage to Canada's economic infrastructure.

- The driest place in Canada is Whitehorse in the Yukon Territory, where annual precipitation is 267.40 millimetres per year.

- St. John's, Newfoundland, is the foggiest city in Canada with 119 days every year with fog. It is also the windiest city, with an average annual wind speed of 23.80 kilometres per hour.

> The sunshine capital of Canada is Medicine Hat, Alberta, with the greatest number of hours of sunshine per year: 2,512.9 hours, based on an eighty-two-city survey by Environment Canada weather expert David Phillips.

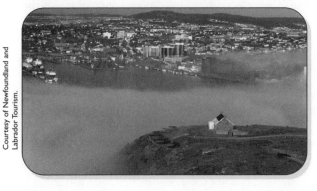

Courtesy of Newfoundland and Labrador Tourism.

A foggy Newfoundland day.

- Quebec is the coldest province in Canada with an average annual temperature of -2.57° C. Nova Scotia is the warmest, at 6.20° C.

Courtesy of Nova Scotia Tourism and Culture.

A stretch of beach in Nova Scotia, Canada's warmest province.

The record for the most intense rainstorm in Canada goes to the downpour that took place at Buffalo Gap, Saskatchewan, on May 30, 1961. Approximately 250 millimetres of rain fell in less than half an hour, washing out roads, eroding fields, and even stripping bark from trees.

The wettest twenty-four hours ever recorded in this country belongs to Ucluelet Brynnor Mines, British Columbia, where 489.2 millimetres of rain fell on October 6, 1967.

- Prince Rupert, British Columbia, is the cloudiest city in Canada, with 6,146 hours per year of overcast skies. It is also the wettest city, with an average annual precipitation of 2,593.60 millimetres of rain and snow.

- The snowiest city in Canada is Gander, Newfoundland, with 443.10 centimetres of annual snowfall.

- Thunder got you spooked? Then move to Nanaimo, British Columbia, which, on average, has thunderstorms on just two days each year.

- It's not always bitterly cold and dark north of the treeline in Canada's Arctic. During the short summer, when daylight is nearly continuous and a profusion of flowers blooms on the tundra, the temperature can reach 30° C.

- The highest humidex reading in Canada in recent history occurred in Windsor, Ontario, on June 20, 1953, when it reached 52.1° C. That measurement of temperature and humidity easily surpassed the highest rating ever in Toronto, which was 48º C, also in 1953.

- Although it can get chilly in Ottawa, where the average winter temperature is -8.9° C, it's only the second-coldest capital city in the world. The number one ranking goes to Ulaanbaator, Outer Mongolia, which has an average daily winter temperature of -22.4° C.

Winterlude festival fun wards off the cold in Ottawa.

Photo by Janis Ray.

SOME FINAL NUGGETS OF NATURE

- The Canadian Shield, a rocky region wrapped around Hudson's Bay, is Canada's largest geographical feature, stretching east to Labrador, south to Kingston on Lake Ontario, and northwest as far as the Arctic Ocean. The shield is made up of rocks that are 3.5 billion years old.

- Wasaga Beach, Ontario, has the world's longest freshwater beach, stretching about fourteen kilometres. More than 2 million people visit the beach each year, which also had the distinction of serving as an airstrip in 1934 for the first flight from mainland Canada to England.

Courtesy of the Town of Wasaga Beach.

Wasaga Beach: once an airstrip, now a popular tourist attraction.

- About 9.7 percent of the land in Canada is privately owned. Fifty percent is provincial Crown land and 40.3 percent is federal Crown land.

- Prince Edward Island is Canada's most densely populated province, with 22.4 people per square kilometre.

- In 1901, Nova Scotia was the first province in Canada to designate an official flower when it chose the mayflower. Nova Scotia is the only province with an official berry, dog, and boat — the blueberry, duck tolling retriever, and *Bluenose II* respectively.

The mayflower, Nova Scotia's official flower.

Courtesy of Communications Nova Scotia.

Canada's largest water control system is the James Bay Project in northern Quebec, which involved the construction of 215 separate dams when it was built

- Canada has 134 native species of trees, and more than 25 percent of them are considered to have medicinal uses. Chewing on willow bark, for instance, is said to help cure headaches because the bark contains salicin, the active ingredient in acetylsalicylic acid.

- Canada is the second-largest country in the world, but only 13 percent of its land is suitable for agriculture. About 6 percent can be used for grazing, while another 7 percent can be cultivated.

TIMELINES

January 4–9

1998: An ice storm hit central and eastern Canada, dropping close to one hundred millimetres of freezing rain. It affected nearly 20 percent of Canada's population, mainly in Montreal and areas around Ottawa and Kingston, making it the most destructive and disruptive storm in Canadian history.

Ice paralyzed Ottawa in 1998.

Photo by Randy Ray.

January 23	**1888:** Natural gas was discovered at Kingsville in southwestern Ontario.
February 2	**1956:** Canada's furry weather forecaster, Wiarton Willie, made his debut in Wiarton, Ontario. Every February 2 since then, the albino groundhog and his successors forecast how many weeks of winter are left.
February 13	**1947:** Vern "Dry Hole" Hunter experienced a long record of worthless holes until he struck oil near Leduc, Alberta. His strike started the Alberta oil boom.
March 16	**1971:** The Ontario government filed a $25-million lawsuit against Dow Chemical of Canada Ltd. for ecological damage to the Great Lakes.
March 30	**1848:** An ice jam at the mouth of the Niagara River blocked Niagara Falls, causing the water to stop running over the falls.
March 31	**1999:** Nunavut, Canada's newest territory, was officially created out of the Northwest Territories.
April 7	**1914:** The western division of the Grand Trunk Pacific Railroad was completed at Nechaco R. Crossing, B.C. The first train arrived at Prince Rupert on April 9.
May 5	**1950:** The Red River in Winnipeg broke through protective dikes and began flooding sections of the city. Within a week more than one hundred thousand Manitobans were forced from their homes.
May 23	**1994:** The common loon became Ontario's official bird. Loons, known for their haunting cry, have been clocked at flying speeds of 120 kilometres per hour.
June 15	**1846:** Under the terms of the Oregon Treaty, the boundary between the United States and what was then British North America was extended along the 49th parallel to the Pacific Ocean.
July 18	**1905:** The Dominion Act created the provinces of Alberta and Saskatchewan, effective September 1.

Edmonton and Regina, respectively, became the capitals on July 20.

July 27

1866: The first transatlantic cable was hauled onto the shores of Heart's Content, Newfoundland, allowing telegraph messages to be transmitted between Europe and North America.

July 29

1916: A devastating forest fire broke out in Matheson, northwest of North Bay, Ontario, taking the lives of between 200 and 250 men, women, and children and destroying six towns, including Matheson and Cochrane.

August 2

1908: A fire scorched the Kootenay Valley of British Columbia, causing $5 million in damage and killing seventy people.

September 12

1991: Canada's Wind Imaging Interferometer (WINDII) was launched aboard NASA's Upper Atmospheric Research Satellite (UARS) to provide new measurements of the physical and chemical processes taking place at altitudes ten to three hundred kilometres above the earth's surface.

September 23

1787: The site of Toronto was purchased from the Mississauga Indians.

September 28

1960: The "Seaway Skyway," a new bridge between Prescott, Ontario, and Ogdensburg, New York, was opened.

October 9

1820: A proclamation announced the amalgamation of Cape Breton Island and Nova Scotia, which took place on October 16.

November 30

1824: Construction began on the Welland Canal, which would join Lake Erie and Lake Ontario.

December 6

1916: The Connaught Tunnel was opened by the CPR, extending eight kilometres through Macdonald Mountain in British Columbia. It is Canada's longest rail tunnel.

QUIZ #13:
SIX TO SAVOUR

1. False. There are more than one hundred.

2. d) It was called Emerald Lake because of its greenish colour.

3. a) Ivy Lea.

4. b) Geologist.

5. a) caribou b) badger c) coyote d) walleye

6. A blizzard.

QUIZ #14:
COAST-TO-COAST QUIZ

1. True. Mt. Logan, at 5,959 metres, is Canada's highest peak.

2. d) No one.

3. Saskatchewan and Alberta.

4. a) Made entirely from wood, the Chateau Montebello was built using 10,000 logs from British Columbia; 500,000 hand-slit cedar roof shakes; 53 miles of plumbing and heating pipes; and 103.5 miles of wooden moulding. It is also known as the world's largest cabin.

5. The Mackenzie, which flows 4,241 kilometres through the Northwest Territories. The St. Lawrence is 3,058 kilometres long.

CHAPTER SEVEN

Canadians of all political stripes love talking, reading, and debating about the people and events that make up Canada's political scene. But while they may be familiar with the faces and issues, what do they know about our rich political heritage and the people who shaped it?

If you already know many of the following facts, you're worthy of the title "Right Honourable."

- When Pierre Trudeau wed Margaret Sinclair in 1971 he became the only prime minister to get married while in office. The couple divorced in 1984.

Courtesy of the National Archives of Canada. PA-163903.

Canada's famous newlyweds.

- In the late 1800s, Minister of the Interior Clifford Sifton attracted immigrants to Canada by flooding "desirable" countries with pamphlets, posters, and advertisements promising free land in Canada's west. In countries where Canada's presence was unwelcome, undercover agents operating as part of the North Atlantic Trading Company were hired to spread word of Canada as the land of opportunity.

- Amor de Cosmos, who served as the second premier of British Columbia from 1872 to 1874, was born William Alexander Smith in Windsor, Nova Scotia. While living in California and working as a photographer at a mining camp, he changed his name to Amor de Cosmos, either to make a new beginning in life or because other Bill Smiths in the camp were mistakenly receiving his mail.

- Richard Bedford Bennett, prime minister from 1930 to 1935, is the only one to hold that post who is not buried in Canada. Bennett is buried in Surrey, England.

- Bennett, Canada's eleventh prime minister, was the first millionaire to hold the country's top office. The New Brunswick native earned his fortune in Calgary on legal fees from the CPR and Hudson's Bay Company and through real estate investments and business ventures such as cement production, power, beer, grain elevators, and a flourmill.

- E.D. Smith was the first senator to resign from office. Smith, the founder of one of Canada's leading food manufacturing companies, based on Ontario's Niagara Peninsula, quit in 1946 because he felt he wasn't worth the money Canadian taxpayers were paying him.

E.D. Smith went from pie fillings to politics.

Courtesy of the National Archives of Canada, PA-805267.

- Sixteen of Canada's twenty-one prime ministers have been lawyers, including Paul Martin, who is a graduate of the University of Toronto Law School. Non-lawyer PMs are Alexander Mackenzie, a stonemason; Mackenzie Bowell, a printer and editor; Charles Tupper, a physician; Lester Pearson, a senior public servant and diplomat; and Joe Clark, a journalist and university lecturer.

Courtesy of the National Archives of Canada, PA-25302.

Courtesy of the National Archives of Canada, C-8100.

Non-lawyer prime ministers Alexander Mackenzie, left, and Mackenzie Bowell, right.

- Rita Johnston became Canada's first female premier in 1991 when she replaced Bill Vander Zalm, who resigned as premier of British Columbia following a scandal. Seven months later, her Social Credit Party was wiped out in an election that cost Johnston her seat. She left politics.

Sir John A. loved a good picnic.

Courtesy of the National Archives of Canada, C-2090.

• Sir John A. Macdonald gets credit for creating the political picnic, for years many politicians' way of glad-handing with as many supporters as possible at a single event. In his bid for re-election in 1878, he sallied forth to towns and villages with a brass band and chicken and ham meals served in local parks, events the citizens would remember for years.

- *Uniting the right.* Long before talks between Stephen Harper and Peter MacKay, Canada's Conservative Party and the Progressive Party merged to become the Progressive Conservative Party in 1941 under leader John Bracken of Manitoba.

Sir John Joseph Caldwell Abbott.

Courtesy of the National Archives of Canada, C-8094.

• Sir John Joseph Caldwell Abbott was the first senator to serve as Canada's prime minister and was also the first PM born in Canada. He was the country's third PM, holding the office from June 16, 1891, to November 24, 1892. A former mayor of Montreal, he became prime minister when Sir John A. Macdonald died while in office.

- In addition to Macdonald, 312 members of Parliament have died while in office since 1867, including Sir John Sparrow David Thompson, who was the country's fourth prime minister when he died on December 12, 1894; John Diefenbaker, the country's thirteenth prime minister, who was a Progressive Conservative backbencher when he died on August 16, 1979; and Liberal-Conservative D'Arcy McGee, who was shot to death in Ottawa on April 7, 1868.

---

1. I was a champion of justice issues including women's rights when I was elected to the House of Commons in 1921. Who am I?

2. Which Canadian prime minister was known as "Old Tomorrow"?

   a) Wilfrid Laurier
   b) John Turner
   c) John Diefenbaker
   d) Sir John A. Macdonald

3. When Canada was formed in 1867, what was the maximum yearly salary a member of Parliament could earn?

   a) $300
   b) $600
   c) $1,200
   d) $3,000

4. What was Joey Smallwood's occupation before he became premier of Newfoundland in 1949?

   a) cab driver
   b) journalist
   c) lawyer
   d) entrepreneur

5. What is the name of the statue on the dome of the Manitoba legislative building in Winnipeg?

QUIZ #15

POLITICAL POSERS

Now it's time for a Question Period of our own. Take our quiz and test your Canadian political IQ. No catcalls, please!

6. What did the federal government outlaw in September 1972 for safety reasons?

    a) firecrackers
    b) open-wheeled go-carts
    c) smoking in airplanes
    d) expense accounts for politicians

7. Where in Canada did women first have the legal right to vote?

    a) Quebec
    b) Ontario
    c) Nova Scotia
    d) Manitoba

8. Where did MPs meet after fire gutted the Centre Block of the Parliament Buildings in 1916?

    a) the East Block at Parliament Hill
    b) Ottawa City Hall
    c) the Museum of Nature
    d) Lansdowne Park

9. Unscramble the following letters to form the name of one of Ontario's Conservative premiers:

    Ibil vidas

10. What was Sir John A. Macdonald's middle name?

    a) Albert
    b) Arthur
    c) Alexander
    d) Allan

 Answers can be found on page 169

LEADERS AND LOSERS

- James S. Woodsworth, a Manitoba Labour MP, put forth a motion in 1923 to disband the RCMP. The motion failed, but several politicians were unhappy with the Mounties at the time, blaming them for the violence in the 1919 Winnipeg General Strike.

- *Maniacal MPs.* During a twenty-seven-hour debate in the House of Commons in 1878, MPs got so wound up in procedural wrangling that they blew tin trumpets, threw sand crackers, sent up toy balloons, sang songs loudly, imitated the crowing of roosters, and threw a wastebasket across the room.

- The airing of daily activities of politicians in Canada's Parliament first took place on October 17, 1977, making Canada the first country ever to broadcast the complete proceedings of its Legislature.

> Blanche Margaret Meagher became Canada's first female ambassador when she was appointed Canada's envoy to Austria in 1961. While in Vienna, she also became this country's representative at the International Atomic Energy Agency.

- Canada's longest serving member of Parliament is Sir Wilfrid Laurier, who was an MP for forty-four years, eleven months, and twenty-three days in the late 1880s and early 1900s. For now, Laurier's record looks pretty safe: the longest serving MP today is Toronto Liberal Charles Caccia, who in early 2004 had sat in the House of Commons for nearly thirty-six years.

- On five occasions sitting prime ministers have lost their own seats during federal elections: Arthur Meighen (1921 and 1926), William Lyon Mackenzie King (1925 and 1945), and Kim Campbell (1993).

Arthur Meighen couldn't hold his seat.

Courtesy of the National Archives of Canada, PA-28132.

Although Sir Charles Tupper holds the record for the shortest term as prime minister (sixty-nine days), three more recent PMs didn't fare much better. John Turner held office for 80 days, Kim Campbell lasted 135 days, while Joe Clark was PM for 273 days.

- When the first provincial legislative building in Toronto was burned down during the War of 1812, politicians met for a time at Jordan's Hotel on King Street.

- In 1951, Louis St. Laurent became the first prime minister to live at 24 Sussex Drive, official residence of Canada's prime minister. The thirty-four-room residence was built between 1866 and 1868 for Joseph Merrill Currier, a prosperous Ottawa lumber mill baron.

Home of Canada's prime minister.

Courtesy of the National Capital Commission.

- Pierre Elliott Trudeau is the first Canadian prime minister born in the twentieth century. Born in Montreal on October 18, 1919, Trudeau held the nation's top political office from April 20, 1968, to June 3, 1979, and from March 3, 1980, until June 30, 1984.

TIMELINES

January 1

1940: The first municipal government of the Northwest Territories was inaugurated in Yellowknife. It remains the chief municipality there today.

January 25

1985: The federal government decreed that all sponsorship of amateur athletic events by tobacco companies would be phased out. The ban was fully implemented by October 1, 2003.

February 2

1848: The first Liberal government in Nova Scotia was elected. James Uniacke became attorney-general and party leader and Joseph Howe became provincial secretary.

February 17

1919: Sir Wilfrid Laurier, Canada's seventh prime minister, died in Ottawa, Ontario, while still a member of the House of Commons.

March 2

1793: Lieutenant-Governor of Upper Canada John Graves Simcoe arrived at the forks of the Thames River in what is present-day London, Ontario, and decided that it should be the future capital of the colony. He later changed his mind and established the capital at York (now Toronto).

The historic forks of the Thames River almost became the site of Ontario's capital.

March 14

1921: Mary Ellen Smith became a minister without portfolio in the British Columbia government, making her the first woman to hold a cabinet post in the British Commonwealth.

April 4

1883: Queen's Park, the main legislative building of the Ontario government, officially opened. Designed by Richard Waite of Buffalo, N.Y., and made from sandstone, the building underwent restoration in the 1990s.

The main legislative building at Queen's park is one of the most recognizable buildings in Ontario.

April 5

1977: Willy Adams of Rankin Inlet, N.W.T., was appointed senator for the Northwest Territories, becoming the first Inuit to sit in Parliament.

May 25

1868: Queen Victoria granted by royal warrant the shield used in the coat of arms of Ontario. The green shield features three gold maple leaves and the Banner of St. George, a red cross on a silver background.

June 3

1909: William Lyon Mackenzie King became the first minister of labour in the newly formed Department of Labour.

June 21

1957: John Diefenbaker became prime minister in the first Conservative administration in twenty-two years. Ellen Louks Fairclough became secretary of state, the first woman to be appointed to the Cabinet in Canada.

Courtesy of the National Archives of Canada, PA-57930.

Dief the Chief.

July 6

1906: Parliament passed the Lord Day's Act, which forbade working on a Sunday and most Sunday transportation. Seventy-nine years later the Supreme Court ruled the act unconstitutional.

July 15

1870: Manitoba joined Canada as its fifth province.

July 20

1871: British Columbia became a province of Canada, influenced partly by a promise from the federal government that a national railway would be built linking B.C. to the rest of the country.

August 18

1988: Legislation permitting the federal government to sell 45 percent of its stake in Air Canada was given royal assent, and less than a month later the share price was set at $8. Canadians began buying and selling Air Canada shares on October 13.

September 1	**1905:** Alberta and Saskatchewan entered the Dominion as the eighth and ninth provinces. George Hedley Vicars Bullies became the first lieutenant-governor of Alberta, and Amedee-Emmanuel Forget the first lieutenant-governor of Saskatchewan.
October 31	**1960:** Walter Pitman became the first MP to be elected as a member of the New Democratic Party, which had formerly been the Canadian Commonwealth Federation.
November 1	**1987:** René Lévesque died of a heart attack in Montreal. He was a former journalist, broadcaster, and provincial Liberal cabinet minister. He was a founder and leader of the Parti Québécois and also served as premier of Quebec.
December 11	**1916:** Saskatchewan voted to abolish liquor stores.
December 13	**1968:** The Legislative Council in Quebec was changed to National Assembly of Quebec.
December 31	**1791:** William Osgoode was appointed first chief justice of Upper Canada.

QUIZ #15: POLITICAL POSERS

1. Agnes Macphail.

© Canada Post Corporation, 1990. Reproduced with permission.

Courtesy of the National Archives of Canada, PA-127295.

Agnes Macphail.

QUIZ ANSWERS

2. d) Sir John A. Macdonald.

3. b) $600.

4. b) Journalist.

5. The Golden Boy.

6. a) Firecrackers.

7. d) Manitoba, where females won the right to vote in January 1916.

8. c) The auditorium at the Museum of Nature, then known as the Victoria Museum.

9. Bill Davis, Ontario's premier from 1971 to 1985.

10. c) Alexander.

CHAPTER EIGHT

THE PUCK STOPS HERE

- The penalty shot, hockey's most exciting play, was introduced in the Pacific Coast Hockey League in 1916–17 by league founders Lester and Frank Patrick. Its first documented use was in a 1922 playoff game when Babe Dye of the Toronto St. Pats failed to score on Harry Holmes of the Vancouver Millionaires.

- Some hockey players have long and illustrious careers without ever winning a championship. And then there's Jean Beliveau. The former Montreal Canadiens captain has had his name engraved on the Stanley Cup more than anyone — seventeen times, ten as a player and seven as an executive.

Jean Beliveau pictured on a Canadian postage stamp.

© Canada Post Corporation, 2001. Reproduced with permission.

- Tetsuhiko Kariya, father of Paul Kariya of the Colorado Avalanche, was born in an internment camp for Japanese Canadians at Greenwood, British Columbia, during World War II. The camps were set up because the federal government was concerned Canadians of Japanese descent would rise up against Canada during the war.

- The first goal scored in Toronto Maple Leafs history came off the stick of George Patterson in a 4 to 1 victory over the New York Americans on February 17, 1927.

Whether with balls and pucks, in the water or on the playing field, Canadians have shone in a variety of sports over the years. In this chapter, we've unearthed a few gems to amaze and entertain anyone with an interest in the world of Canadian sports. We couldn't resist starting and ending this section with hockey, but you may be surprised by some of Canada's exploits in the Olympics, football, golf, and baseball. We've also served up a couple of quizzes to test your sports IQ.

- Mario Lemieux of the Pittsburgh Penguins is the only player in the NHL to score his fiftieth goal of the season on a penalty shot. The goal came on April 11, 1997, against Florida Panthers goalie John Vanbiesbrouck.

- The Hockey Hall of Fame in Toronto is located in an old Bank of Montreal building that is said to be haunted by a ghost. A former teller at the bank killed herself in the 1950s because of an unrequited love affair, and her ghost has been seen on several occasions.

Canada's Hockey Hall of Fame is said to be haunted by a ghost.

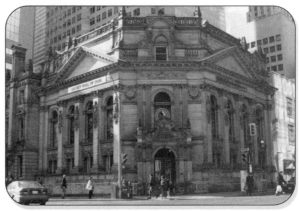

The phantom player. In 1974 the Buffalo Sabres chose as their second-last pick in the annual hockey draft a player named Taro Tsujimoto — but no such player existed. He was a figment of the imagination of one of the Sabres' public relations officers. Once the prank was discovered, the Sabres were not allowed to select a real player in Tsujimoto's place.

- Jack Darragh and Mike Bossy are the only NHL players to score back-to-back Stanley Cup–winning goals. Bossy, of the New York Islanders, scored in 1982 against the Vancouver Canucks and in 1983 against the Edmonton Oilers. Darragh accomplished the feat in 1920 and 1921 when the Ottawa Senators knocked off the Seattle Metropolitans and the Vancouver Millionaires.

- In the 2003–2004 season, the National Hockey League's 728 players hailed from twenty-four different countries: 52.1 percent were Canadian; 32.4 percent were from outside North America; and 15.5 percent were Americans. Ten years ago, the breakdown was Canadian, 78.3 percent; non-North American, 8.7 percent; American, 13 percent.

- *Taller, heavier, older.* In the 2003–2004 season, the average height, weight, and age of an NHL player was 6'1", 204.6 pounds, and 27.9 years of age. Thirty years ago, it was 5'11", 186.1 pounds, and 26.2 years old.

- Craig Ramsay of the Buffalo Sabres is the last NHL player to play a full season without drawing a single penalty. He went penalty-free in 1973–74, when he played seventy-eight games and recorded twenty goals and twenty-six assists.

- Teammates have scored their fiftieth goals of a season in the same game only twice in NHL history, and both times it was Pittsburgh Penguin players. On March 21, 1993, Mario Lemieux and Kevin Stevens each scored number fifty of the season, and on February 23, 1996, Lemieux and teammate Jaromir Jagr each notched their fiftieth goals.

- In the history of the National Hockey League only eight players have scored seventy goals or more in a season: Phil Esposito, Wayne Gretzky, Brett Hull, Mario Lemieux, Jari Kurri, Alexander Mogilny, Teemu Selanne, and Bernie Nicholls.

THE PUCK'S THE THING

- Researchers at the Hockey Hall of Fame speculate that early hockey players, most of whom were college educated, referred to the disk as a "puck" in reference to the sprite from Shakespeare's *A Midsummer Night's Dream* who appeared and disappeared without warning. Others say "puck" derives from the Irish word meaning "to strike." The term "puck," as used in hurley, an Irish game similar to hockey, refers to hitting or striking the ball with the stick.

Lord Stanley, Canada's sixth governor general, is best known for donating the trophy that bears his name, but in 1888 he also was the voice on the first known sound recording made in Canada, entitled "A Message to the President of the United States of America."

The theme for *Hockey Night in Canada,* one of the country's most recognizable tunes, was written by Delores Claman back in 1967. She's also known for writing the "Ontari-ari-ario" tune, "A Place to Stand."

- Hockey pucks have been made of rubber since about the 1880s, but in the beginning most were wooden. In Nova Scotia, where many experts believe the first hockey games in Canada took place, players would also use other objects for pucks, such as the heels of boots, flattened tin cans, lumps of coal, and frozen horse droppings, which they called "horse puckies" or "horse apples."

Pucks, once wooden, are now made of rubber.

Courtesy of Harry Johnson, Canterbury Rusty Blades, Ottawa.

- Not just any rubber disk makes it into a National Hockey League game. Rule 24 from the NHL's official rule book says game pucks must be made of vulcanized rubber or other approved material that is one inch thick and three inches in diameter and shall weigh between five and one-half ounces and six ounces. All pucks used in competition must be approved by the league's rules committee.

- The average number of pucks used in an NHL game is thirty-five. Pucks are kept frozen at 18° F and, according to the NHL rule book, a supply must be kept at the penalty bench under the control of one of the regular off-ice officials or a special attendant.

- *Producer of the pucks.* The official supplier of NHL game and practice pucks is In Glas Co., a Sherbrooke, Quebec, company that provides the league with more than 240,000 pucks every season. In Glas Co. also manufactures replica pucks, plastic and wooden miniature hockey sticks, key chains, pins, water bottles, and pennants for the NHL, Team Canada, and the American Hockey League.

BET YOU DIDN'T KNOW

- Although Marilyn Bell made her name nationally by becoming the first person to successfully swim across Lake Ontario, she was also the youngest person to swim the English Channel and the Strait of Juan de Fuca.

- Arnie Boldt was the first athlete with disabilities to be elected to Canada's Sports Hall of Fame. Boldt, an Osler, Saskatchewan, native who lost a leg at age three in an accident, won gold in the long jump and high jump at the International Olympiad for the Disabled held in Toronto in 1976.

- Bishop's University's sports teams are called the Gaiters because of the school's Anglican origins. Some divinity graduates at the Quebec university wore traditional garb, including a gaiter, which is a legging made from either canvas or leather. Although the university's teams had been referred to in the past as the Purple and White, the name Gaiters was officially adopted in 1949.

- Bruce Kirby of Ottawa designed the Laser sailboat in 1969. Just shy of fourteen feet long, the one-person craft went into production in 1971 in Pointe Claire, Quebec, and early in the twenty-first century approximately 250,000 had been sold. Kirby has competed for Canada in several Olympic Games in sailing events.

They're at the post! The horse race starting gate is a Canadian invention, designed in the early 1900s by Philip McGinnis, a racetrack reporter from Huntingdon, Quebec. The device prevented arguments when horses started prematurely.

Photo by Margo Kirby.

Bruce Kirby, inventor of the Laser.

Photo by Bruce Kirby.

A Laser sailboat on the move.

Based on rate of participation, golf is Canada's top sport, followed by hockey and baseball. About 7.4 percent of Canadians hit the links every year, 6.2 percent chase a puck around the ice, and 5.5 percent try to hit a home run.

- On September 11, 1839, the first track and field meet in Canada was held at Caer Howell grounds near Toronto.

- Ben Weider, who along with his brother Joe built one of Canada's largest health and fitness enterprises, is recognized as an expert in Napoleonic history. He's co-written three books on the subject and helped prove that Napoleon was poisoned to death.

Ben and Joe Weider with Arnold Schwarzenegger, once a spokesman for their bodybuilding techniques.

Photo by Albert Busek, courtesy of Ben Weider.

- *Canadian connection.* When Canadian James Naismith invented basketball in Springfield, Massachusetts, in 1891, five of the eighteen players in that first game (there were nine a side back then) were Canadian. They helped spread the sport in Canada when they returned for Christmas vacations that year.

- Injuries suffered by divers led Canadian Olympic diving coach Herb Flewwelling to invent the bubble machine in 1971. By mixing air with water and creating mounds of bubbles the device softens the impact when divers hit the water.

- The Fox 40 pealess whistle has been used by referees in the Canadian Football League and the National Basketball Association, as well as by coast guards worldwide and during several Olympics since it was invented in 1987 by Ron Foxcroft, a part-time basketball referee from Hamilton, Ontario.

Courtesy of Fox 40 International Inc.

The Fox 40 Classic Whistle.

- Thirteen Canadians have won the famed Boston Marathon race, including Ronald J. MacDonald, who won the second race ever in 1898; Jacqueline Gareau, this country's only female winner; and Andre Viger, who won the wheelchair division three times after it became an official event. Gerard Côté was Canada's greatest champion, winning the race four times in the 1940s.

GOING FOR GOLD

- George S. Lyon of Canada won the gold medal in golf at the Olympics in St. Louis in 1904. It was the last time golf was played in the Olympic Games.

- Although two-time Olympic gold medallist Percy Williams is rightly recognized by many as one of Canada's greatest athletes, he was twice beaten in the mid-1920s by Cyril Coaffee. In 1922, Coaffee ran the 100-yard dash in 9.6 seconds, tying the world record and setting a Canadian standard that wouldn't be bettered for twenty-five years.

Courtesy of the National Archives of Canada, PA-150993.

Percy Williams, foreground, on the run.

- In the 1904 Olympics, Canada, represented by the Galt (Ontario) Football Club, captured the gold medal in soccer when it defeated a U.S. team from St. Louis 4 to 0. There was, however, little representation from Europe at that Olympics.

- *The Big Owe.* Montreal's Olympic Stadium was originally supposed to cost $120 million, but flawed workmanship and a poor design, among other problems, will see the price tag balloon to about $3 billion by the time it's paid off in 2006.

Montreal's $3-billion Olympic Stadium.

Courtesy of Montreal Olympic Park.

- At the 1934 British Empire Games, Phyllis Dewar of Moose Jaw became the first Canadian woman to win four gold medals for swimming, a record that stood until 1966.

- *Jumps of a different kind.* Winning Olympic gold in figure skating in 1948 didn't mean the end of Barbara Ann Scott's sporting career. The popular Olympic champion from Ottawa excelled in equestrian events when she was in her mid-40s.

- He's by no means a well-known athlete in Canadian sports history, but Spike Smallacombe of Toronto holds the distinction of being the first from this country to win a gold medal at the Commonwealth Games. Smallacombe hopped, stepped, and jumped his way to gold in the triple jump in 1930 in what were then known as the British Empire Games.

Mark each of the following True or False:

QUIZ #16

QUICK QUIZ

Okay, we've fed you a few tanta-lizing tidbits; now it's your turn to see just what you know about sports in Canada.

1. Jacques Plante was the first NHL goaltender to wear a mask.

2. Babe Ruth hit his first professional home run in Toronto.

3. The Edmonton Eskimos was the first Western Canadian team to play in a Grey Cup.

4. Canada's first Olympic gold medal in ice hockey was won during the Summer Games.

5. The nickname "gee-gee," used by University of Ottawa sports teams, is a slang term for groundhog.

6. Kent Douglas was the last member of the Toronto Maple Leafs to win the NHL's Calder Memorial Trophy as rookie of the year.

 Answers can be found on page 197

AT THE PLATE

•   Historians have validated a record of a baseball game that took place in 1838 in the southwestern Ontario community of Beachville. The game was described some years afterward by Dr. Adam Ford, who remembered attending it as a boy. That match is notable because it occurred one year before Abner Doubleday supposedly "invented" the game in Cooperstown, New York.

•   The Toronto Blue Jays aren't the first major league baseball team to have that nickname. In 1944–45, the Philadelphia Phillies were also known as the Blue Jays, but the name didn't stick.

- Baseball players can thank Toronto-born Art Irwin for introducing the baseball glove to the sport. Prior to his invention, fielders caught baseballs with their bare

A Canadian invention that caught on.

hands, but when Irwin broke two fingers in a game in 1883, he came up with a prototype for a glove that he used successfully. Other sources say another Canadian, Phil Powers, may have invented the glove five years earlier.

Tip O'Neill, an outfielder from Woodstock, Ontario, in the 1880s, still boasts the highest major league baseball batting average ever. During the 1887 season he batted .492. Walks were counted as part of the average then, but even when they are deducted, O'Neill still batted an impressive .435.

- Jack Graney of St. Thomas, Ontario, was the first baseball payer to get a hit off Babe Ruth in the major leagues. Ruth started his career as a pitcher. As for Graney, he played fourteen seasons and then became the first ex-ballplayer to broadcast a game on radio.

- Still with Jack Graney, this innovator also changed the sport of baseball in 1916 when he became the first batter to wear a number on his uniform. Graney batted .250 during his major league career.

- Ferguson Jenkins, the Hall of Fame baseball player from Chatham, Ontario, was considered by some to be the best control pitcher in the sport's history. But before he became a pro baseball player, he played junior hockey and basketball for the Harlem Globetrotters.

Ferguson Jenkins pitching against the Montreal Expos.

Courtesy of the National Archives of Canada, PA-209772.

- *Is there a doctor on the diamond?* Dr. Ron Taylor, former team physician for the Toronto Blue Jays, has four World Series rings, two awarded to him when the Jays won the series in 1992 and 1993, and two from his previous career as a major league relief pitcher with the 1964 St. Louis Cardinals and 1969 New York Mets.

FOOD FORE THOUGHT

- When George Lyon of Toronto won a gold medal in golf for Canada in the 1904 Olympic Games he was the lone Canadian in a field of seventy-five competitors. All others were Americans. Legend has it that he accepted his medal by walking on his hands to the presentation.

- Dawn Coe-Jones of Campbell River, British Columbia, recorded the second double-eagle of her career in 1993. She was one of only two LPGA players with two career double-eagles. The other was Sherri Turner.

- The Links O'Tay Golf & Country Club in Perth, Ontario, has the oldest golf course on a permanent site in Canada. When it opened in 1890 it had three holes, which the golfers repeated three times to make up a nine-hole course; eventually it grew to nine separate holes, and early in the new millennium it expanded to a full eighteen.

> A golfer who found a 203-gram meteorite on the Doon Valley Golf Course near Kitchener, Ontario, on July 12, 1998, was rewarded with a year's worth of free green fees. The space stone, which had earlier landed on the sixth tee, narrowly missed another golfer.

> When Mike Weir of Bright's Grove, Ontario, won the Masters Golf Tournament in Augusta, Georgia, in April 2003, he was not only the first Canadian to claim the green jacket, he was also the first left-handed golfer to win the title.

- The Rundle Golf Course in Edmonton takes its name from an unusual source. It's named after Reverend Robert Terrill Rundle, who arrived in the area in 1840 and later established the first permanent missionary of any religion in Alberta.

- Murray Tucker, a native of Mitchell, Ontario, was Canada's first Master Professional golfer. Tucker, who died in June 2002, was inducted into the Canadian Golf Hall of Fame for his contributions to the game, which included the presidency of the Canadian Professional Golfers' Association in 1959–60. He won the Ontario Open in 1950 and the Ontario PGA in 1958.

Karl Keffer, the only Canadian to win the Canadian Open.

Courtesy of Canadian Golf Hall of Fame and Museum.

- Karl Keffer of Tottenham, Ontario, is the only Canadian-born player to win the Canadian Open golf championship. Keffer, who is a member of the Ontario and Canadian Golf halls of fame, took the title in 1914. Pat Fletcher, a Canadian citizen but a native of England, won the tournament in 1954 at the Vancouver Point Grey Golf Club.

TOUCHDOWN TRIVIA

- Students from McGill University in Montreal introduced the game of rugby, with its oblong ball, to their Harvard counterparts in 1874, who up to that time played only with a round ball. The Americans adopted the game, and it eventually evolved into the football that is now played throughout the country.

- The Grey Cup, trophy of the Canadian Football League championship, cost $48 to make in 1909. It was supposed to be awarded to amateur football clubs only, but professional players began showing up on teams at least as early as the 1930s.

- Johnny Reagan of the Winnipeg Blue Bombers was the first black quarterback in the Canadian Football League. He played quarterback and other positions for the Bombers in 1947.

- The origin of the Huskies nickname for University of Saskatchewan sports teams had nothing to do with the dog. The players on the football teams of the early 1900s were more muscular and larger than other athletes, and thus referred to as "husky." Today, however, the nickname has evolved to refer to the dog.

> The average career for a player in the Canadian Football League is about 2.1 years, or approximately 36 games. The average National Hockey League player is in the league for 4.5 years, or about 370 games.

> During the pre-season in 1961, the Hamilton Ti-Cats of the CFL tangled with the Buffalo Bills, of the old American Football League, in Hamilton, in a game using Canadian rules. The Ti-Cats won 38 to 21, and after the game the AFL refused any more cross-border matches.

- *Road to ... Vancouver.* When the B.C. Lions of the CFL were formed in 1954, the new club was partially financed by selling a limited number of memberships for $20 apiece. Among those buying memberships were entertainers Bing Crosby and Bob Hope.

- The Senators' name is not only associated with the National Hockey League team in Ottawa. Back in the 1920s, the Ottawa Rough Riders football team changed its name to Senators for a couple of years and won two Grey Cups during that time.

- The Winnipeg Blue Bombers football team takes its name from the nickname of former heavyweight champion Joe Louis, who was known as the Brown Bomber. The Winnipeg squad was given the moniker by an American reporter who saw them play an exhibition game against the University of North Dakota in 1936.

> Pamela Anderson's acting career was launched in 1989 when a Jumbotron camera focused on her at a B.C. Lions football game in Vancouver. Clad in a Labatt's t-shirt, her fulsome figure caught the attention of beer company executives and she went on to do commercials, appear in *Playboy* magazine, and join the cast of the TV show *Baywatch*.

In an age when high sports salaries are the norm, Canadian Football League players earn an average of about $45,000 a year. The average NFL player, by comparison, makes about thirty-five times that amount annually.

- The Toronto Argonauts experienced financial troubles in 2003; that was nothing compared to what they were up against in 1879. The football club, which at that time was affiliated with its rowing counterpart, didn't play a single game all year because the players had sustained muscle injuries from several rowing competitions.

- Larry Haylor, coach of the University of Western Ontario Mustangs football team, is the winningest coach in Canadian intercollegiate football history. In September 2003 he notched career win number 154, breaking a tie with David (Tuffy) Knight.

Larry Haylor, with all his wins, has plenty to smile about.

Courtesy of the University of Western Ontario.

QUIZ #17

SPORT STUMPERS

1. What trophy do the champions of Canadian university football win?

   a) Grey Cup
   b) Vanier Cup
   c) Macdonald Cup
   d) Pearson Cup

2. According to a 2000 Statistics Canada report, what's the most popular exercise activity among Canadians?

   a) walking
   b) swimming

c) cycling

e) gardening

3. What do Canadian athletes Robert Kerr, George Hodgson, Ethel Catherwood, and Marnie McBean have in common?

4. What was the name of Toronto's first professional basketball team, which played in the 1946–47 season?

a) Huskies

b) Towers

c) Metros

d) Maple Leafs

e) Bobcats

5. Where is the Canadian Baseball Hall of Fame located?

a) Saskatoon, Saskatchewan

b) Fredericton, New Brunswick

c) Surrey, British Columbia

d) Cornwall, Ontario

e) St. Marys, Ontario

6. Name the two football teams that joined in 1950 to form the Hamilton Tiger-Cats.

What was Georges Vezina's nickname?

Courtesy of the National Archives of Canada, C-29549.

7. Hockey legend Georges Vezina had an unusual nickname. What was it?

a) The Chicoutimi Cucumber

b) Le Grand Orange

c) Old Needle Nose

d) The Gaspe Grabber

8. The regular season football game between the Hamilton Ti-Cats and the Ottawa Rough Riders on September 14, 1958, was unusual for what reason?

a) It featured a woman place-kicker

b) It was the highest scoring game in history

c) It was played in Philadelphia

d) It was the first nationally televised game

185

9. In what city did Wayne Gretzky play his last game in the NHL?

   a) Ottawa
   b) Toronto
   c) New York
   d) Chicago
   e) Edmonton

10. Which one of the following sports was invented in Canada?

   a) volleyball
   b) tennis
   c) skiing
   d) five-pin bowling

 Answers can be found on page 198

SPORTS OF ALL SORTS

> Curling has been played in Canada since the mid-eighteenth century, when Scottish soldiers introduced the game here. The first curling club established in North America was in Montreal in 1807.

- The last harness race at Toronto's Greenwood racetrack took place on New Year's Eve, 1993, at 5:07 p.m. The event was won by a three-year-old pacer named Kirk Henley, driven by Steve Condren.

- Though the sport of fencing has been established in Canada since the late eighteenth century and national fencing championships have been in place for one hundred years, Canada has yet to win an Olympic medal in the sport. Canadians have done well, however, at the Commonwealth and Pan-Am Games.

- When Marilyn Bell became the first person to swim across Lake Ontario, she took more than twenty hours to accomplish the task. But while the lake is thirty-two miles across, Bell had swum the equivalent of more than forty miles because currents prevented her from swimming in a straight line.

- The first karate school in Canada opened in Toronto in 1956. The school was operated by Canadian-born karate master Masami Tsuruoka, who helped spread the sport across this country and founded the National Karate Association in 1964.

- Chuckwagon races have been a part of the Calgary Stampede since 1923. In that first year, the competitors not only had to drive their wagon, but also had to finish up by unhitching their team of horses and firing up a cook stove.

Courtesy of the Calgary Stampede.

Chuckwagon races are a Stampede tradition.

- Before he made his name as a clothes salesman for big and tall men, George Richards of Toronto was a professional wrestler. He competed throughout Canada and the U.S., including at Maple Leaf Gardens. When the Gardens first opened in 1931, Richards sold programs to make ends meet.

- The first national gymnastics championship in Canada was held at the CNE in Toronto in 1923, but it wouldn't be until 1954 that the competition was open to women.

- The Edmonton Grads are the most successful team in Canadian sports history. The women who made up this champion basketball team were all graduates of McDougall Commercial High School in Edmonton. The team, coached by Percy Page, was formed in 1915 and over the next twenty-five years won 502 games and lost only 20.

- Ringette, the game played on ice with a stick and hollow rubber ring, was developed in North Bay, Ontario, in 1963 by Sam Jacks. The game has become popular internationally, and the first world championships were held in the Ottawa suburb of Gloucester in 1990.

Ringette is a Canadian game.

Courtesy of Ringette Canada.

- There are two sets of Astroturf at Toronto's Skydome, one for baseball, the other for football. The 152 strips of turf are five metres wide and range from fifteen to seventy-seven metres in length. The surface of the turf can endure up to eighty times more use than real grass.

- When Thunder Bay, Ontario's Horst Bulau won the 1979 world junior ski jumping championships, he became the first Canadian to win a world Nordic ski title. Bulau had thirteen World Cup wins after that.

- Marilyn Bell was not the only swimmer in the chilly waters of Lake Ontario in September 1954 when she became the first woman to swim the lake. Also in the water were American marathoner Florence Chadwick and Canadian Winnie Leuszler. Leuszler quit after only a few hours; Chadwick was pulled from the water when she became ill.

- In 1970, Canadian skier Betsy Clifford of Old Chelsea, Quebec, was the youngest skier in the his-

CSM #71.72.1 Canadian Ski Museum, Le Musée canadien du ski, Ottawa, ON.

tory of Alpine skiing to win a gold medal at the World Championships in Val Gardena, Italy, in the Giant Slalom. She was sixteen at the time.

Betsy Clifford speeds to victory in Val Gardena in 1970.

- Two Canadians have been world singles handball champions: Joey Maher of Toronto in 1967 and Merv Deckert of Winnipeg in 1984.

- James Naismith of Almonte, Ontario, the inventor of basketball, has often been referred to as James A. Naismith. Trouble is, Naismith had no middle name. When asked what it stood for he once joked that he was the first James Naismith in his family, and the A was to reference the generations alphabetically. Although there are probably ten James directly descending from him, none took the next letter.

- George Dixon of Halifax won the world bantamweight title on June 27, 1890. He won $2,000 for his efforts, which marked the first time a black man won a world boxing title.

- Steve Nash, superstar player for the Dallas Mavericks of the National Basketball Association, became the first Canadian ever named to the NBA All-Star team in February 2001.

- In 1927, George Young of Toronto, at the age of seventeen, became the first person to swim across California's Catalina Channel. The teenager completed the twenty-two-mile swim in just over fifteen hours and claimed a $25,000 prize.

- When Vancouver's bid for a National Basketball Association franchise was first endorsed in 1994, the team was known as the Mounties, not the Grizzlies. However, the RCMP stepped in and asked that its nickname not be used for the team.

- The first Arctic Games, held in Yellowknife in 1970, drew participants from Alaska, the Yukon Territory, and the Northwest Territories. The games, held every two years and featuring such sports as skiing, hockey, badminton and traditional Inuit games, now draws competitors from Nunavut, Greenland, and parts of Russia.

- During a 1966 bout at Maple Leaf Gardens, George Chuvalo became the first professional boxer to go the distance with American boxer Muhammad Ali. Chuvalo was never knocked out in ninety-seven career heavyweight fights.

QUIZ #18

CUP QUIZ

The Stanley Cup, the supreme trophy in all of hockey, has been hoisted by some of the most famous names in the history of the game. Let's see how much you know about hockey's most elusive prize.

1. What was original name of the Stanley Cup?

   a) the Upper Canada Cup
   b) the Dominion Hockey Challenge Cup
   c) the Macdonald Trophy

Lord Stanley's cup.

Photo by Randy Ray.

2. Approximately how much did it cost to make the first Stanley Cup?

   a) $100
   b) $50
   c) $1,050

3. Leading up to the 2003–2004 season, which Canadian team last won the Stanley Cup?

4. True or false? The Stanley Cup has been to the White House.

5. What was the Montreal Victorias claim to fame in Stanley Cup history?

   a) They won the cup with a team consisting of only seven players
   b) They won the cup in 1899 but refused to accept it
   c) They were the first team to accomplish a "hat trick" by winning the cup three years in a row

6. What do Brendan Shanahan, Brett Hull, and Howie Morenz have in common?

   a) All have scored Stanley Cup–winning goals
   b) All were captains when their teams won the cup
   c) None has ever played on Stanley Cup–winning teams

7. Where was the first Stanley Cup made?

   a) Toronto
   b) Halifax
   c) Sheffield, England
   d) Boston, Massachusetts

8. Which team was the first winner of the Stanley Cup?

   a) Toronto Arenas
   b) Montreal Amateur Athletic Association
      c) Ottawa Senators

 Answers can be found on page 199

TIMELINES

January 13

1971: Frank Mahovlich was traded by the Detroit Red Wings to the Montreal Canadiens for three players, Mickey Redmond, Guy Charron, and Bill Collins. Mahovlich later helped the Canadiens upset the Boston Bruins in seven games in the 1971 quarter-finals.

February 1

1971: The Philadelphia Flyers of the National Hockey League sent goaltender Bernie Parent and a second-round draft pick to Toronto for goalie Bruce Gamble and forward Mike Walton. Two years later, Toronto traded Parent back to Philadelphia, where he helped the Flyers win two Stanley Cups.

February 7

1976: Darryl Sittler, captain of the Toronto Maple Leafs, scored six goals and four assists, helping the Leafs beat the Boston Bruins 11 to 4. It was the greatest individual scoring performance in one game in NHL history.

February 23

1906: Tommy Burns of Hanover, Ontario, became the first Canadian heavyweight boxing champion of the world by winning a twenty-round decision over Marvin Hart.

March 31

1923: King Clancy, while playing for the Ottawa Senators, played every position, including goal, in a Stanley Cup game. The Senators beat the Edmonton Eskimos 1 to 0.

May 2

1964: Northern Dancer became the first Canadian-born horse to win the Kentucky Derby. Northern Dancer would also win the Preakness and the Queen's Plate.

June 10

1938: Cyclist extraordinaire Torchy Peden was given a gold-plated bicycle in Victoria, British Columbia, to recognize his triumph at the World Professional Six-Day Bicycle Championship.

June 24

1968: Sandra Post from Oakville, Ontario, became the first rookie and first foreign player to win the U.S. Ladies' PGA Championship.

July 7	**1904:** The Winnipeg Shamrocks won a gold medal in lacrosse in the Olympics in St. Louis. Canada won gold in lacrosse again four years later.
July 17	**1976:** The Olympic Games in Montreal were officially opened by Queen Elizabeth II. These were the first Games held on Canadian soil.
August 1	**1932:** High jumper Duncan McNaughton of Cornwall, Ontario, won the gold medal in the high jump at the Olympics in Los Angeles. He cleared six feet, six inches.
August 16	**1969:** The first Canada Summer Games, held in Halifax–Dartmouth, Nova Scotia, were opened.
August 30	**1953:** Doug Hepburn of Vancouver won the world heavyweight weightlifting championship in Stockholm, Sweden.
September 2	**1904:** Etienne Desmarteau became the first Canadian to win an Olympic gold medal while competing for Canada when he came in first in the fifty-six-pound throw in St. Louis. Four years earlier, Canadian George Orton had won gold, but he was competing for the U.S. because Canada didn't have a team.
September 4	**1876:** Ned Hanlon of Toronto won the world rowing championship in Philadelphia. Hanlon was a leading athlete in the late nineteenth century and is a member of the Canadian Sports Hall of Fame.
September 17	**1932:** Sandy Somerville of London, Ontario, became the first Canadian to win the U.S. amateur golf championship. Somerville was also the first golfer to score a hole-in-one in the Masters tournament in Augusta, Georgia.
October 11	**1952:** The first telecast of a hockey game, between the Detroit Red Wings and the Montreal Canadiens, was transmitted in French on CBFT.
October 23	**1990:** Wayne Gretzky became the first National Hockey League player to score two thousand points.

November 1	**1952:** The first hockey game telecast in English was broadcast on CBLT in Toronto. The game featured the Toronto Maple Leafs and the Boston Bruins.
November 17	**1968:** Playing in Rome, George Knudson and Al Balding were the first Canadians to win golf's World Cup.
November 19	**1969:** Toronto Argonauts head coach Leo Cahill made his famous statement that "it will take an act of God to beat us Saturday" after his team defeated the Ottawa Rough Riders in the first of a two-game total point clash. The Rough Riders, led by quarterback Russ Jackson, did beat the Argos 32 to 3 and went on to the Grey Cup.
December 1	**1960:** Gordie Howe became at that time the NHL's all-time leading scorer with 1,092 points.
December 4	**1909:** The University of Toronto defeated Parkdale Canoe Club 26 to 6 to win the first Grey Cup.
December 31	**1968:** Herve Filion set a world horseracing record when he won 407 races in one year.

OVERTIME

- The Memorial Cup, awarded to Canada's top major junior team, was donated in 1919 as the John Ross Robertson Memorial Cup. Robertson had been the president of the Ontario Hockey Association in the early 1900s and donated the trophy as a tribute to the many hockey players who served and died in World War I.

- Syl Apps, one of the great hockey players in Toronto Maple Leaf history, also won a gold medal in the pole vault in the 1934 British Empire Games in London, England.

- The Hart Memorial Trophy, given to the NHL's most valuable player, was donated to the league in 1923 by Dr. David Hart, father of Cecil Hart, a former manager of the Montreal Canadiens. Wayne Gretzky won the trophy a record nine times during his career.

- Though he was the National Hockey League's most prolific scorer until Wayne Gretzky came along, Gordie Howe's professional career had a slow start. In his first three NHL seasons, Howe scored only seven, sixteen, and twelve goals respectively.

- As a ten-year-old playing in Brantford, Ontario, Gretzky scored 378 goals in 72 games, setting the stage for future stardom.

© Canada Post Corporation, 2000. Reproduced with permission.

The Great One was a star at age ten.

- Only three players have led the NHL in scoring while playing on teams that finished in last place. According to hockey trivia expert Liam Maguire, they were Joe Malone of the Quebec Bulldogs in 1919, Dave Schriner of the New York Americans in 1937, and Max Bentley of the Chicago Black Hawks in 1947.

- Frank McGee of the Ottawa Silver Seven, an early 1900s hockey team, scored a record fourteen goals in the second of a two-game total goal series against the visiting team from Dawson City in defence of the Stanley Cup in the 1905–06 season. The final score in that game was 23 to 2.

• When Conn Smythe bought the Toronto St. Patricks hockey team in 1926 he wanted to change the name. He was scouting some players on a team that called itself the East Toronto Maple Leafs, and he liked the name enough to adopt it for his new squad. The Toronto Maple Leafs debuted in February 1927 wearing the now-familiar blue and white uniforms.

Bobby Baun was known as the "boomer" for his crunching bodychecks.

• Today's multi-million-dollar contracts mean most NHL players no longer hold down jobs outside hockey in the summer. That wasn't the case before the days of big contracts, though. In the 1960s, Toronto Maple Leafs player Bobby Baun worked in a gravel pit to make ends meet; fellow Leaf Tim Horton sold classified advertising; and Marcel Bonin, who played with the Detroit Red Wings, Boston Bruins, and Montreal Canadiens, worked part-time wrestling bears.

• The first National Hockey League goalie to be credited with a goal was Billy Smith of the New York Islanders. The marker came on November 28, 1979, in the Islanders' 7 to 4 loss to Colorado. Since then, seven other netminders have scored goals, including Ron Hextall of the Philadelphia Flyers and Martin Brodeur of the New Jersey Devils, who have each scored twice.

• Goaltenders cannot take faceoffs in National Hockey League games. One NHL rule says a hockey team consists of players and goalies, and another says faceoffs are to be taken by players. The bottom line? Forwards and defencemen can take face-offs; netminders cannot.

- It may sound strange, but the Ottawa Senators have won six Stanley Cups. Of course, we're talking about the earlier incarnation of the franchise, which existed between 1903 and 1934. That Senators team moved to St. Louis in 1934.

- Bobby Hull, a star forward with the Chicago Black Hawks in the 1960s and early 1970s, was the first National Hockey League player to earn $100,000 in yearly salary. But it took a bitter holdout in 1968 to convince his bosses he was worth it.

- When Bobby Hull notched his fiftieth goal against the Detroit Red Wings in March 1966 he became the National Hockey League's first two-time fifty-goal scorer.

- The Detroit Red Wings were not always named the Red Wings. The hockey team started out as the Cougars, and later changed its name to the Falcons. In 1933, owner Jim Norris changed the name to the Red Wings in tribute to the Winged Wheelers, a Montreal Athletic Association team he played for in the 1890s.

Gretzky versus Lemieux. Researchers at Texas A & M University, who studied hockey players from 1948 onward, concluded that Mario Lemieux would be rated the best-scoring forward over Wayne Gretzky. Analyzing several factors, the researchers said if both had played at their peak at the same time, Lemieux would have outscored "The Great One" by six points a season.

QUIZ #16:
QUICK QUIZ

1. False. Clint Benedict of the Montreal Maroons wore a mask during the 1929–30 season.

2. True. As a player with the Providence Grays, Ruth hit his first professional home run against the Toronto Maple Leafs on September 5, 1914.

QUIZ ANSWERS

3. True, in 1921.

4. True, at the 1920 Games in Antwerp.

5. False. It's a slang term for horse.

6. False. It was Brit Selby in 1966. Douglas won the trophy three years earlier.

QUIZ #17:
SPORT STUMPERS

1. b) The Vanier Cup.

2. a) Walking.

3. They all won gold medals at the Summer Olympics.

4. a) Huskies.

5. e) St. Marys.

6. The Hamilton Tigers and the Hamilton Wildcats.

7. a) He was known as the Chicoutimi Cucumber, because he was thought to be a cool customer while playing in goal.

8. c) It was played in Philadelphia because of a labour dispute with Hamilton stadium officials. Until the 1990s, it was the only CFL game played south of the border.

9. c) New York. His last game in Canada was in Ottawa.

10. d) Five-pin bowling was invented in Toronto in 1905 by Thomas Ryan.

QUIZ #18:
CUP QUIZ

1. b) The Dominion Hockey Challenge Cup.

2. b) $50.

3. The Montreal Canadiens in 1993, when they defeated the Los Angeles Kings to take the final, four games to one.

4. True, during the presidencies of George Bush, Bill Clinton, and George W. Bush.

5. c) They won the cup three years in a row in 1896, 1897, and 1898.

6. a) All have scored Stanley Cup–winning goals.

7. c) Sheffield, England.

8. b) The Montreal Amateur Athletic Association in 1893. The team declined to accept the cup because of an alleged slight, but they accepted the prize a year later.

CHAPTER NINE

TRIVIA TREASURE TROVE

We've dug deep into our chest of trivia treasures for a wealth of gems dealing with everything from chubby Canadians and tall buildings to famous names and popular automobiles.

AND THE TRIVIA JUST KEEPS ON COMING

• In the fall of 1969, after the liberalization of Canada's criminal code, the first gay and lesbian group on a Canadian university campus was formed at the University of Toronto. Jearld Moldenhauer, a research assistant in the faculty of medicine, placed a four-line classified advertisement in the university's Varsity newspaper asking others to join the University of Toronto Homophile Association. The first meeting drew fifteen men and one woman.

• The number of bison in Alberta rose by 250 percent between 1996 and 2001 to nearly 80,000 animals on 950 ranches. The latest statistics show that in total the Canadian herd, which is concentrated on the Prairies, is about 145,000 bison on about 1,900 farms.

Photo by Ella Wright.

A bison in Waterton Park, Alberta.

• There are nearly 3 million obese Canadians aged twenty to sixty-four in Canada, an increase of 24 percent from the mid-1990s. Fifteen percent of Canadians are now overweight, compared to 13 percent less than a decade ago, says the Canadian Community Health Survey.

• About 46 percent of the rebels in the Upper Canada Rebellion of 1837 were farmers, and the majority of them were either American-born or had American parents.

- Although the FLQ gained most of its notoriety during the October Crisis of 1970, the organization had been around since the early 1960s. The FLQ claimed responsibility for about two hundred bombings in the seven years prior to the October Crisis.

BIG, BIGGER, BIGGEST

- Toronto's CN Tower, at 553.33 metres, is the world's tallest free-standing structure. The $63-million tower and tourist attraction has also been classified as one of the Seven Wonders of the Modern World by the American Society of Civil Engineers.

- The *Paul R. Tregurtha*, also known as the "Queen of the Lakes," is the largest ship to ever travel Great Lakes waters. The $60-million ship measures 1,013 feet, 6 inches in length, about the same as three football fields. It was built in 1981 as the *William J. Delancy* in Lorain, Ohio, by the American Shipbuilding Company and was renamed *Paul R. Tregurtha* in 1990. The vessel is 105 feet wide, 56 feet deep, and is capable of carrying up to 68,000 tons of cargo in her five cargo holds.

> At an oil sands surface mine near Fort MacMurray, Alberta, Syncrude has excavated more soil than was moved to build the Great Wall of China, the Great Pyramid of Cheops, the Suez Canal, and the world's ten largest dams combined.

Photo by Jim Hoffman, courtesy of www.wellandcanal.ca.

> Paul R. Tregurtha was chairman of the Interlake Steamship Company in 1990 when the ship was given his name.

- Canada once laid claim to producing the world's largest cheese. Made in Perth, Ontario, the cheese weighed almost ten thousand kilograms (twenty-two thousand pounds). It was shipped by train for display at the Chicago World's Fair in 1893.

- The Inco Super Stack, which services Inco's Copper Cliff nickel, copper, and precious metals smelter at Sudbury, Ontario, is believed to be the world's tallest smokestack, at 375 metres (1,250 feet) high. It went into operation on August 21, 1972, as a way of improving air quality in the area, where mining is the major industry.

The Inco Super Stack.

Courtesy of Inco Ltd.

One of the largest outdoor pipe organs in the world is found at the Amphitheater at the Chautauqua Institution in Chautauqua, New York. The organ, which has 5,628 pipes, was donated to the institution in 1907 by Toronto's famous Massey family and was built by the Warren Organ Company of Woodstock, Ontario, at a cost of $40,000.

- The cost of building the Canadian Pacific Railway in the 1880s was $150 million, which in today's dollars is the equivalent of about $4.5 billion. About 59 percent of the tab was borne by taxpayers.

- When construction of the CN Tower began in February 1973, the base of the excavation was below the level of nearby Lake Ontario. Water was kept out of the working area by sixty wells drilled around the edge of the site and operated by a pair of diesel engine pumps.

- Work on the Trans-Canada Highway began in 1950 and was completed in 1970 at a cost of more than $1 billion. Those who drive it from end to end will travel 7,821 kilometres.

1. Although contraceptives didn't become legal in Canada until 1969, the first birth control clinic in the country opened in 1932. Where was it located?

    a) Hamilton
    b) Vancouver
    c) Winnipeg
    d) Halifax

2. Which of the following games was *not* invented in Canada?

    a) Trivial Pursuit
    b) Scrabble
    c) Balderdash
    d) Scruples

3. In which war did the battle of Vimy Ridge take place: World War I or World War II?

4. The February 1963 issue of *Imperial Oil Review* reported that a Canadian had invented a vehicle that was a "kind of scooter mounted on toy tracks and which growls like a runaway dishwasher." What kind of vehicle was it?

    a) a snowmobile
    b) an all-terrain vehicle
    c) a mini-bike
    d) a hovercraft

5. Which province boasts Canada's longest coastline: Newfoundland or British Columbia?

 Answers can be found on page 218

Answers can be found on page 218

QUIZ #19

QUICK QUIZ FIVE-PACK

So, which province lays claim to Canada's longest coastline? When did the battle of Vimy Ridge take place, and what do you know about Canadian board games? Find out with this quick quiz.

WHAT'S IN A NAME?

> Labrador takes its name from Joao Fernandes, a Portuguese landowner, or "labrador." Fernandes reached Greenland in 1499, which as a result was called Labrador. In the sixteenth century, the name was transferred to the east coast of North America, where it has since remained.

- On St. Lawrence's Day in 1535, Jacques Cartier gave the saint's name to one small bay near the mouth of the St. Lawrence River. By 1600, it was used to describe the entire river.

- The Plains of Abraham, site of the famous Seven Years War battle between British Major-General James Wolfe and French Lieutenant-General the Marquis de Montcalm, is named after Abraham Martin, who farmed the land in the mid-seventeenth century. The September 13, 1759, battle was won by the British.

- *From limestone to lilies.* Butchart Gardens, a fifty-five-acre landscaped garden north of Victoria, British Columbia, is named for wealthy cement manufacturer Robert Butchart and his wife, Jennie, who built a home and decided to beautify an adjacent limestone quarry in the early 1900s. Today, the site is a popular tourist attraction.

From quarry to gardens.

Courtesy of the Butchart Gardens, Victoria, B.C., Canada.

- The original tower at the Centre Block of Parliament Hill in Ottawa was known as the Victoria Tower. Following a major fire in 1916, the existing version of the tower was built and known temporarily as the Tower of Peace and Victory. In

1927, it was officially named the Peace Tower, following correspondence between the tower's architect and Prime Minister Mackenzie King.

The Peace Tower in Ottawa has had several names

Photo by Andrew Ray.

- During World War I, the Ontario community of Berlin changed its name to Kitchener when the loyalty of its large German-Canadian population was questioned. The new moniker was in honour of Lord Horatio Kitchener, a British war hero who at the start of the war was appointed Secretary for War by the British government. Kitchener died in 1916 when his ship was sunk.

- *Gone to the dogs.* Bowser, a small community on the east side of Vancouver Island, is named for William Bowser, who was premier of British Columbia from 1915 to 1916. In the 1930s, the local hotel had a dog named Mike that was trained to deliver beer to tables.

- Lethbridge, Alberta, was first called Fort Whoop-Up by European settlers and then renamed Coal Banks after the discovery of the mineral of the same name in the area. The town boomed with the opening of

> Gold prospectors in Canada's north became known as "sourdoughs" because the bread, which doesn't require yeast, was a popular staple in mining camps. Mining veterans survived the cold winters because they knew how to make the bread. Being called a "sourdough" was a sign of respect for enduring the often harsh conditions.

the North Western Coal and Navigation Company and was renamed in 1885 in honour of the firm's president, William Lethbridge.

- Melville, Saskatchewan, 130 kilometres northeast of Regina, was named after Sir Charles Melville Hayes, a former president of the Grand Trunk Pacific Railway who died aboard the *Titanic* when it sunk near Newfoundland in April 1912.

- Kingston, Ontario, was first known as King's Town. Following the American Revolution in 1785, an influx of United Empire Loyalists settled in what was then known as Cataraqui. They renamed it King's Town, which eventually evolved to Kingston. It officially became a town in 1838, and in 1841 it served as the first capital of the United Canadas.

Kingston was once King's Town.

- In 1950, the most popular baby names for boys and girls in Canada were Robert and Linda. By 1970, Michael and Lisa topped the list, and when the new millennium arrived, it was Matthew and Emily.

- Prince Edward Island is affectionately referred to by locals as "The Island," but over the years it has also been called "Spud Island," "The Garden of the Gulf," "The Million-Acre Farm," and the "Cradle of Confederation." Its earliest settlers, the Micmac, called it Abegweit, which means "Cradle in the Waves."

- Although most Canadians associate Meech Lake with the constitutional accord negotiated there by former prime minister Brian Mulroney, the actual lake is a wooded area that's frequented by nudists and cottagers. The lake is named for Asa Meech, a Congregationalist minister from New England who lived there in the nineteenth century.

- The southwestern Ontario community of Ingersoll is named for Major Thomas Ingersoll, the father of Laura Secord, the War of 1812 heroine who warned British troops in 1813 of a surprise attack by the Americans. Ingersoll is the site of Ontario's first cheese factory.

- "Kabloona" is an Inuit word for white Canadians who live in the far north. And "Kabloonamuit," which means "people of the white man," is the word for those Inuit who try to imitate white people and their ways.

> According to the Newfoundland Liquor Corporation, the name "screech" for the rum made in that province originated when an American soldier stationed there in World War II let out a howl after taking a swig. A sergeant arrived on the scene to ask about "that ungodly screech" and was told by a Newfoundlander, "'Tis the rum."

---

1. The early 1960s slogan "Put a tiger in your tank" was the brainchild of what automobile fuel company?

   a) Supertest
   b) Esso
   c) Fina
   d) Texaco

Tiger fuel.

2. True or false? In 1903, when Canada's first automobile clubs were founded, there were fewer than two hundred cars in the country.

QUIZ #20

YOU AUTO KNOW II

Another chance to test your knowledge of Canada's highways and byways.

3. In 1900, F.S. Evans set a speed record for the sixty-kilometre trip by automobile between Toronto and Hamilton. How long did it take him?

    a) ninety minutes
    b) two hours
    c) two hours and forty-five minutes
    d) three hours and twenty minutes

4. What city hosted Canada's first automobile race?

    a) Montreal
    b) Halifax
    c) Winnipeg
    d) Toronto
    e) London

5. What is Canadian racecar driver Earl Ross's claim to fame?

    a) He was once NASCAR's Rookie of the Year
    b) He won the first Can-Am race in the 1960s
    c) He won a race against an airplane in 1917
    d) He was the first Canadian to compete in the Indy 500

6. The Peck was an electric car built in Toronto from 1911 to 1913. What was the company's slogan?

    a) "This car Pecks a punch."
    b) "Keeps pecking."
    c) "A Peck of a smooth ride."
    d) "Drive a Peck today."

7. What is the name of the scenic drive between Banff and Jasper national parks?

8. True or false? Ontario was the first province to establish a Department of Highways.

9. In 1991, Petro-Canada announced one of the following. Was it:

    a) a new consumer-friendly credit card
    b) Canada's first customer rewards program

c) the sale of its shares to the public
d) development of a revolutionary touch-free car wash system.

10. The University of British Columbia's sports teams have the same name as a popular sports car. What is it?

Answers can be found on page 219

TRY THESE ON FOR SIZE

• The design of Toronto's city hall was the result of a competition in 1957–58 that attracted more than 530 entries from architects around the world. The winning design was by the Finnish architect Revell, despite a report that argued the two towers would be functionally impractical.

The design contest for Toronto's city hall attracted hundreds of submissions from architects around the world.

- When Kapuskasing was designed in the early 1900s it was known as the "Model Town" of Ontario's north because it was built like a wheel with spokes.

- The carillon in the Peace Tower at Parliament Hill consists of fifty-three bells made in Croydon, England. The largest bell weighs 10,160 kilograms and sounds the note E. The smallest bell weighs 4.5 kilograms and is pitched to the A note.

- *Chilling story.* On February 23, 1995, two-year-old Karlee Kosolofski of Regina survived the lowest body temperature ever recorded, 14.2° C, when she was accidentally locked out of her house for six hours when the outdoor temperature was –22.2° C.

- Charles Atlas, the American strongman who sold new bodies to countless skinny kids from ads on the back of comic books, retired to Morrisburg, Ontario, where he amused local boys by straightening horseshoes.

LIFE IN CANADA

- By 1930, when 70 percent of the people in this country had electricity, Canadians had already claimed the title of being the largest per capita users of electricity in the world.

However you pour it, Canadians love their salt.

- Canadians are the largest consumers of salt in the world — on average, about 360 kilograms per person per year.

- In the 1920s, making cheddar cheese was a way of life in rural Ontario. It was the first job off the farm for thousands of farm boys and was the main source of cash income for 35 percent of Ontario farmers.

- Suicide kills an average of 3,700 Canadians a year. About 80 percent of victims are men.

- In 1989, the average Canadian household saved $6,250 a year. But early in the twenty-first century, families were socking away only $1,664 annually.

> In 2004, more than eighty thousand children in Canada were being educated in private homes. That compares to about two thousand in 1979.

- A baby born in Canada can look forward to living 79.3 years, on average; that's three years longer than twenty years ago, according to Statistics Canada. Only people in Japan (81.1 years) and Iceland (79.7 years) can expect to live longer than the average Canadian.

- About 31 percent of adult Canadians are involved in some kind of volunteer work. In most years about 7.5 million Canucks volunteer a combined 1.1 billion hours of their time.

- Before 1900, besides Sundays, the concept of a holiday in Canada was generally limited to days such as the Christian holy days of Good Friday and Christmas. As technology spread, time was saved, and at the turn of the century the idea of spending a few "working days" away from work for leisure began to emerge. People began using the term "weekend" for the first time, and began taking part in activities other than going to a place of worship; some had a half-day off work on Saturday.

> On average, Canadian Internet users receive 123 e-mails per week. Fifty-two percent of these e-mails are spam — double what it was in June 2002.

THE WEIRD, THE WONDERFUL, AND THE WACKY

- Camels imported from the U.S. were used as pack animals along the Cariboo Trail during the B.C. gold rush of the 1860s. The camels, however, had trouble handling the rocky trails and eventually were set free to roam in the wild.

The Haskell Free Library and Opera House on the Vermont-Quebec border has the unique distinction of having a stage in Canada while the seats are in the United States. Construction on the building started in 1901 thanks to a bequest by Martha Stewart Haskell, a Canadian, to honour her husband, Carlos, an American.

• In 1913, more than four hundred thousand immigrants arrived in Canada, the highest total of any year. The years 1912, 1911, and 1910, in that order, were the three other years that saw the highest wave of immigration to Canada.

The CN Tower: built to last.

• The CN Tower in Toronto is built to withstand two-hundred-mile-per-hour winds, but if it ever toppled it would crash through the SkyDome, the Metro Convention Centre, the Gardiner Expressway, or almost to Union Station, depending on which direction it fell.

• Of the ten tallest office towers in Canada, six are located in Toronto, including the highest, First Canadian Place, at 72 storeys and 952 feet. Of the other four, two are located in Montreal and two in Calgary.

WHEN DISASTER STRIKES

- Fifty-five people died on May 26, 1896, when the Point Ellice Bridge between Victoria, British Columbia, and Esquimault collapsed, sending riders and pedestrians into the water below. It was the worst accident in Canadian transit history.

- The worst avalanche in Canada took place in British Columbia in 1910 at Rogers Pass, derailing a train and killing sixty-six people.

- A dust explosion at a coal mine in Hillcrest, Alberta, on June 19, 1914, killed 189 miners.

- On December 6, 1917, the French munitions ship *Mont Blanc* collided with the Belgian relief ship *Imo* in Halifax Harbour, causing an explosion that killed more than sixteen hundred people and seriously injured nine thousand more. Six thousand people were left homeless, and damage was estimated at $50 million.

- Between 1918 and 1925, an outbreak of Spanish Influenza affected all regions of the country, killing more than fifty thousand Canadians.

- A crash of an Arrow airplane on December 12, 1985, at Gander, Newfoundland, is the worst aviation disaster in Canadian airspace. The crash killed 256 people. The Swissair Flight 111 crash near Peggy's Cove, Nova Scotia, on September 2, 1998, was the second worst tragedy, killing 229.

- The Swissair crash at Peggy's Cove took more than lives. Also lost were a painting by Pablo Picasso, a kilogram of diamonds, and fifty kilograms of banknotes.

> Canada's first recorded marine disaster took place on August 29, 1583, when the Delight was wrecked off Sable Island, about three hundred kilometres southeast of Halifax. Eight-five lives were lost.

> *Off the rails.* A Mississauga, Ontario, train derailment in October 1979 forced the evacuation of 220,000 people after poisonous chemicals were spilled just west of Toronto. Fortunately, no one was killed.

TRIVIA, TRIVIA, AND MORE TRIVIA

- *Teacher crunch.* The number of teachers in Canada's publicly funded schools declined to 240,000 in 2003 from 284,000 in 1991–92, but during the same period the number of students increased by more than 200,000. To make matters worse, approximately 45 percent of the current teaching force will be eligible for retirement by 2008.

- The smallest, oldest jail in North America is found in Rodney, Ontario, southwest of London. Built in 1890 and now a tourist attraction, the 24.3-square-metre jail had two cells. Others have challenged Rodney's claim, but the town has refuted them.

There is little elbow room in North America's smallest jail.

Photo by Sue Bandeen.

- Although Montreal eventually staged the world's fair, Expo '67, during Canada's Centennial, it wasn't supposed to happen. Moscow had been awarded the fair for 1967, but pulled out because of high costs associated with staging the event. Montreal got the gig instead.

- Nearly 50 percent of deaths among Canadian children and teenagers aged ten to nineteen are due to external events, most commonly motor vehicle accidents. Among teens fifteen to nineteen, suicide is the second-leading cause of death, accounting for about 20 percent of teenage deaths.

- Canadians are about five times more likely to be coffee drinkers than tea sippers. Although tea used to be more popular about fifty years ago and is gaining popularity, Canadians much prefer coffee.

- *Changing times.* In 1929, less than 4 percent of Canadian women worked outside the home. By early in this century, however, times had changed, and more than 60 percent were in the labour force.

- Toronto's Union Station train terminal is built from twenty-seven-metric-tonne blocks of Indiana limestone. The existing terminal, officially opened in August 1927 on Front Street between Bay and York, is the fourth version of Union Station.

> The United Church of Canada was created on June 10, 1925, in Toronto when the Methodist, Presbyterian, and Congregationalist churches of Canada joined forces.

The current Union Station has been a focal point for travellers in Toronto since 1927.

TIMELINES

January 1

1911: Cadet training in high schools was made compulsory in Canada.

February 8

1980: After stepping down as Liberal leader in November 1979, Pierre Trudeau returned on this date and led the Liberals to a majority election victory, winning 146 seats.

February 16

1985: Award-winning novelist Marian Engel died in Toronto after a battle with cancer. Her novel *Bear* won the Governor General's Award in 1976.

March 4

1910: The Royal Canadian Navy was established.

April 6

1886: Vancouver was incorporated as a city.

April 19

1900: Roland Michener, the twentieth governor general of Canada, was born in Lancombe, Alberta. Michener served as a Conservative MP and high commissioner in India and brought a more informal tone to the job of Queen's representative.

Courtesy of the Office of the Secretary to the Governor General.

Roland Michener was Canada's twentieth governor general.

May 1

1921: The Quebec government took control of the sale of liquor in the province.

May 9

1906: Lethbridge and Medicine Hat, Alberta, were incorporated as cities. Today, Lethbridge is Alberta's third-largest city, while Medicine Hat is an important industrial centre.

June 1

1909: Governor General Lord Grey donated the Grey Cup, a trophy to be awarded to the best amateur football team in Canada. Several years later professional teams started competing for it.

Courtesy of the National Archives of Canada, C-1017.

Lord Grey.

June 14	**1919:** John Alcock and Arthur Brown completed their successful flight across the Atlantic and landed in Clifden, Ireland, making them the first to fly across the ocean. Their flight had begun in St. John's, Newfoundland.
July 1	**1873:** Prince Edward Island joined Confederation.
July 17	**1812:** British soldiers captured Fort Michilimackinac from the Americans in one of the first clashes in the War of 1812.
August 25	**1785:** Fleury Mesplet published the first edition of the *Montreal Gazette,* the oldest newspaper still in existence in Canada.
August 26	**1961:** Prime Minister John Diefenbaker opened the Hockey Hall of Fame in Toronto and announced the establishment of annual grants worth $4 million for amateur sports in Canada.
September 3	**1825:** The Halifax Banking Company (Collins Bank) opened its doors. It was founded by Enos Collins, Samuel Cunard, and five others.
September 4	**1984:** Brian Mulroney swept to victory as Canada's new prime minister in a federal election in which his Progressive Conservative Party won 211 seats, the largest majority in Canadian history.
September 28	**2000:** Pierre Elliott Trudeau, Canada's fifteenth prime minister, died in Montreal, Quebec. He held office from April 20, 1968, to June 4, 1979, and from March 3, 1980, to June 30, 1984.
October 5	**1984:** Marc Garneau became the first Canadian in space aboard the space shuttle *Challenger.*
October 20	**1855:** Toronto became the new capital of Canada.
October 27	**1998:** *The National Post* newspaper was launched with the goal of becoming a national newspaper.
November 22	**1917:** The National Hockey League was formed, with Frank Calder as the first president.

December 3	**1960:** Edmonton International Airport opened.
December 20	**1792:** Regular mail service was established between what is now Canada and the United States.

QUIZ ANSWERS

QUIZ #19: QUICK QUIZ FIVE-PACK

1. a) Hamilton.

2. b) Scrabble was invented in the U.S.

3. World War I, in April 1917.

4. a) It was the first snowmobile, invented by Armand Bombardier in 1959 in Valcourt, Quebec.

5. At 28,956 kilometres, the coastline of Newfoundland is the longest of any Canadian province. British Columbia is second with 25,725 kilometres. The distances include mainland and all significant islands.

Courtesy of Newfoundland and Labrador Tourism.

Newfoundland has Canada's longest coastline.

QUIZ #20:
YOU AUTO KNOW II

1. b) Esso.

2. True.

3. d) He made the trip in three hours and twenty minutes.

4. c) Winnipeg hosted Canada's first automobile race in 1901.

5. a) He was NASCAR's rookie of the year in 1974.

6. b) "Keeps pecking."

7. The Icefield Parkway.

8. False. Quebec's DOH was created in 1914. Ontario followed suit in 1916.

9. c) On July 3, 1991, the company sold its first shares to Canadians.

10. Thunderbird.

ACKNOWLEDGEMENTS

As with all of our previous books, *Pucks, Pablum &
Pingos* could not have been completed without the help
of the many people who answered our questions or who
pointed us to sources when we were stumped.

We're grateful to numerous government officials,
public relations officers, company and association
spokespersons, and archivists who shared information or
told us about others who might.

Though we could never name them all, we'd like to
acknowledge the many authors and historians who have
written about things Canadian long before we have and
who left behind a wealth of information and ideas for
us to tap into.

We owe a big thanks to all our writing colleagues
and friends at the Periodical Writers Association of
Canada and elsewhere for mentioning trivial items
whenever they came upon something they thought
might interest us.

As always, we want to acknowledge Pat Tripp and
Arthur McClelland at the London Public Library and
the excellent staffs and collections at the University of
Western Ontario and, in Ottawa, the Ottawa Public
Library, the National Archives, the National Capital
Commission, Canada Post, and the Parliamentary
Library. They never fail to deliver the goods when we
come calling.

We also want to give a special thanks to the Royal
Canadian Legion, the Hospital for Sick Children, the
Canadian War Museum, Statistics Canada, the
Department of Veteran's Affairs, Heritage Canada, Ford
Motor Company of Canada, various sports associations

and leagues, including the National Hockey League, and provincial and municipal tourism and other government departments across Canada that were generous with information and photographs.

Friends, colleagues, and family members who continue to offer ideas, tidbits, and encouragement include John Firth, Ed Janiszewski, Arthur McCudden, Bryan Ray, Harold Wright, Harold Johnson, Richard Patterson, David Phillips, Sheila Brady, Liam Maguire, Carl Dow, and Louise Rachlis. Thank you all.

A heartfelt thank-you goes out to Canadian trivia lovers everywhere who have supported the six previous books we have written and who have visited our Web site at http://www.triviaguys.com.

We must also pass along our gratitude to several newspaper editors across the land, at papers such as *The Globe and Mail, Kitchener-Waterloo Record, Ottawa Sun, Brandon Sun, Winnipeg Free Press, London Free Press, Toronto Star, Metro Today, Toronto Sun, Sherbrooke Record, Ottawa Citizen,* and *Forever Young,* who faithfully publish the trivia columns and quizzes we churn out in our never-ending quest to inform and entertain.

As always, we appreciate the special attention we have received from the folks at The Dundurn Group in Toronto, particularly Tony Hawke, Kirk Howard, Jennifer Scott, Jennifer Bergeron, Andrea Pruss, Beth Bruder, and Mike Millar. This is our fifth book with Dundurn, where we have always found the staff to be professional and enthusiastic. The occasional free dinners and drinks on their tab are nice, too.

Finally, we're ever thankful to our wives, Janis Ray and Catherine Blake, for their support, advice, and ideas about our latest endeavour. It is to Janis and Catherine, the Ray boys, Chris, Andrew, and Marcus, and our faithful home office canine companions, Watson and Duffy, that we dedicate this book.

INDEX

ABOUT THE AUTHORS

Mark Kearney   **Randy Ray**

Photo by Catherine Blake

Photo by Janis Ray

Mark Kearney, who has worked as a journalist for more than 26 years, lives in London, Ontario. **Randy Ray** lives in Ottawa and has been a journalist for more than 27 years. Together, as Canada's Trivia Guys, they have won writing awards and written several best-selling trivia books. Visit their website at www.triviaguys.com.